Bridging the Gaps in Global Communication

by Doug Newsom

Blackwell
Publishing

BLACKWELL PUBLISHING
350 Main Street, Malden, MA 02148-5020, USA
9600 Garsington Road, Oxford OX4 2DQ, UK
550 Swanston Street, Carlton, Victoria 3053, Australia

First published 2007 by Blackwell Publishing Ltd

1   2007

Library of Congress Cataloging-in-Publication Data

Newsom, Doug.
    Bridging the gaps in global communication / by Doug Newsom.
        p. cm.
    Includes bibliographical references and index.
    ISBN-13: 978-1-4051-4411-7 (hardback : alk. paper)
    ISBN-10: 1-4051-4411-4 (hardback : alk. paper)
    ISBN-13: 978-1-4051-4412-4 (pbk. : alk. paper)
    ISBN-10: 1-4051-4412-2 (pbk. : alk. paper) 1. Communication, International.
2. Intercultural communication. I. Title.

    P96.I5N487 2006
    302.2—dc22

                                                    2006022220

A catalogue record for this title is available from the British Library.

Set in 10.5/13pt Dante
by Graphicraft Limited, Hong Kong
Printed and bound in Singapore
by COS Printers Pte Ltd

The publisher's policy is to use permanent paper from mills that operate a
sustainable forestry policy, and which has been manufactured from pulp
processed using acid-free and elementary chlorine-free practices. Furthermore,
the publisher ensures that the text paper and cover board used have met
acceptable environmental accreditation standards.

For further information on
Blackwell Publishing, visit our website:
www.blackwellpublishing.com

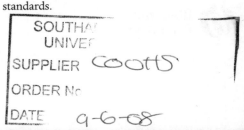

Contents

Contents

Preface

People who are connected to the world and exposed to different cultures and perspectives are far more likely to develop the imagination of 11/9 (Fall of the Berlin Wall). People who are feeling disconnected, for whom personal freedom and fulfillment are a utopian fantasy, are more likely to develop the imagination of 9/11 (Attacks on World Trade Center in New York, Pentagon in Washington, D.C., and crash in Pennsylvania of plane assumed to be destined for the White House.) (T. L. Friedman 2005: 463).

Ever wonder why *Time* Magazine's Asian edition carried a picture of Mohammad with Angel Gabriel in its story of the Muslim Faith? Why do you suppose McDonald's failed to explain that part of the secret to its flavorful fries was beef broth in the recipe? Both situations resulted in international embarrassment and apologies. Since both are global corporations, one would expect them to know better.

Another global icon, Coca-Cola, failed to respond promptly to contaminated supplies in France and Belgium that made customers, including children, ill. Why? Locals had to clear releases with corporate headquarters in Atlanta, Georgia, USA with no allowances for time zone differences.

The Economist got sued for libel in Singapore and apologized as well as paying a fine to keep out of court. Singapore has a sedition act and the government can't be criticized, even mildly.

When President George Bush launched the war on terrorism and called it a "crusade," he started an international avalanche of ill will. Travelers to India might be cautioned that a head gesture that resembles a Western "no," is probably a sign of understanding or agreement. Verbal and nonverbal expressions have cultural meanings. Even well-intentioned translations may not take into consideration idiomatic expressions of another language.

This book is not a first-aid kit to keep you globally safe from such glitches, but learning to think differently helps. You are by virtue of technology a global citizen. Get used to it. Get comfortable with it. What this book is designed to do is to make you aware.

The first four chapters talk about global sources of information and their systems of communication. When you are reading something from the USA's Associated Press, you are getting news from a free enterprise system, but news from other wire services, like those from France and Tokyo, are owned by the government. Some governments own outright all of the news media there, not just the wire services. Much of what is on the Internet is unmediated information, so you're getting opinion and news often in an indiscernible mix. The concepts, economics and politics of information are important for you to know to evaluate information.

The other ten chapters give you some theoretically underpinnings for interpersonal and public information and the cultural context in which information is both given and received. This includes news and advertising as well as the information from public relations sources. Legal and ethical issues are raised. There's a chapter too on such miscommunication and its consequences that you encountered in the first few paragraphs of this preface. The book ends with some ideas about your developing a worldview both personally and professionally.

List of Figures

Part I

Global Sources and Systems of Communication: Concepts, Economics, and Politics

Information is distributed globally today in real time.

People are so connected by technology that you can call a friend in Stockholm, Sweden, on your cell phone. (Whether you should or not may depend on the time of day or night and the time zone you are calling from.)

Email messages are sent from almost anywhere in the world and received in nearly any setting today. Most public facilities and educational institutions have "live" or wireless reception areas.

Personal channels of communication make it easy to keep in touch with friends, family and business 24/7.

Mass communication channels are on the same schedule. You can go into hotel rooms all over the world and get CNN on television.

Organizations, profit and nonprofit, keep up with employees anywhere in the world by intranet and their business contacts – buyers, suppliers, distributors and investors – by Internet.

The communication tools are there, but what makes a difference in the transfer of understanding are the sources and systems, their concepts, economics, and politics. Concepts are important because there are two levels of decision making in any culture: individual and personal. A culture may determine, though, which dominates. The government system's structure provides an infrastructure for communication and provides for or restrains individual freedom to communicate. The economic aspect is another consideration. Information may be commercially based, where messages are competitive, or it may be government based and supportive of government systems.

Technology has the global society so awash in information from satellite delivery systems that, layered on top of local sources – both mass and interpersonal – to even start making sense of such cacophony, it is necessary to organize the information into some meaningful context. Sorting out facts from opinion is a start, but even facts often conflict. Critical thinkers examine sources of information. Although the information may not originate with the source, it helps to examine two major sources – interpersonal channels and extrapersonal, or public channels. Public channels include mass media as well as corporate and nonprofit media.

What is communicated is intended for both individual and communal decision making. Some societies are more dependent on one than the other, but in either case, making some meaning of messages has to be done by individuals. The context for their attention to and use of information depends on their cultural, social, political, and economic circumstances.

Cultures convey values that influence how people react to and act on information. Exposure to information often is dependent upon government structures and their stability. Structures and stability vary and, within them, individual freedoms and responsibilities. Economies are either commercially based, competitive, or government-based, supportive. An individual evaluating the significance of a message with economic consequences ranks it according to personal experiences with economic structure or structures. In a competitive marketplace information about the economy is more likely to get attention than in a government-based system where the individual may be somewhat protected from economic turbulence unless the political system becomes unstable. These factors are the consideration of chapters 1–4.

Chapter 1

Organization of Information

[T]he great challenge of our time will be to absorb these changes in ways that do not overwhelm people but also do not leave them behind. (T. L. Friedman 2005: 46)

Objectives

- To realize that people can only respond to information – including visuals – within their own realm of experience.
- To accept the limitations of genuine understanding of others.
- To consider the sources of information in interpersonal and public channels and the consequences for public discourse.
- To engage in thoughtful analysis of what we know and what we think we know.

An Argentinean college student attending a southwestern US university was appalled to find that sidewalks were uncommon except in the business districts. She was puzzled that everyone drove even short distances until she realized that walking in the streets was risky. A Singaporean student studying in the midwest US was confounded by the lack of mass transportation. Well, there were busses, but few riders, schedules somewhat less than dependable and access to many places just not available. Only a few cities in the USA have sufficient mass transportation, bus and rail, so that you don't need a car.

Students from other countries with those experiences here know that is why people in the USA have cars and consequently use so much fuel. People without those experiences don't. Londoners even ask their US friends why they don't walk or ride mass transit. "Because we can't" is a response they understand cognitively, but not emotionally.

We accept information then try to find a frame of reference for it to aid comprehension. If that frame is lacking, there is a disconnect. We have information that we accept intellectually, but can't relate to and therefore really don't understand.

Is there any wonder that when people in other countries watched the televised attacks on the Twin Towers of the World Trade Center in New York they interpreted the events in so many different ways? Some were told, and believed, that this was a scene created by Hollywood as propaganda, and not real. Others who did accept what they saw on television as real thought all of the people in the towers were white Americans, probably Christians and Jews and thus persecutors of members of their faith, so this was in a sense deserved and perhaps an act of divine intervention. Some Caucasians who remember that Americans leveled their cities during World War II thought perhaps it was the USA's turn to experience such a disaster. Those who resent the USA's global leadership were not unhappy to see the giant attacked.

These people had a frame of reference, but they also had an association, learned or experienced, that conditioned their response.

We organize new information based on what we know or think we know.

Sources of our information have a great deal to do with our knowledge and interpretation. Interpersonal channels, family and friends, are very influential due to their high credibility. Public channels, or extrapersonal channels, include government or quasi-government. These can be anything from libraries and schools to facilities such as postal authorities, hospitals, fire and police facilities. Information acceptance from these channels depends both on access and acceptance of their reliability.

The delivery of information depends upon systems, either mass communication or organizational systems that can be profit or nonprofit groups. "An information system," says Christine L. Nystrom (2002: 179), "is that form of human organization made possible by a certain combination of characteristics in the form, magnitude, velocity, direction, and accessibility of information."

Sources of Information

Two primary sources of information available to us have considerable impact on both behavior and belief. *Interpersonal* channels are family and friends that provide both information and ideas. They often affect the way we think about things and because we want to preserve the closeness of these relationships, they often affect our behavior too.

Extrapersonal channels are as pervasive in our lives as friends and family, but they are likely to be public channels, usually governmental. If the post office tells you what forms you need to get a package delivered to your friend in time for a birthday, you trust that information and the source. The police put out information about how to protect your home and property. The fire department alerts you to dangers in your residence that you perhaps were unaware of. You learn to trust information often based on experience. The package gets there on time for your friend's birthday, so that's a good experience. The level of trust for government sources of information often comes from experience or from the recommendation of others close to you about whether or not that agency can be trusted. A friend might say, "If you have an accident, think twice before you call the police because they often try to get cash from you instead of writing you a ticket." While that may have been that person's experience, you don't know the level of corruption there unless you hear more information. Yet, you may trust the information because a friend told you the story.

Interpersonal channels

Our most credible sources of information are family and friends. One of the reasons is familiarity and another is the face-to-face communication that usually occurs. Face-to-face is the most persuasive form of communication and the telephone is next, followed by mail, now generally email.

Familiarity always occurs in a relationship because of expectations that develop. Continuing the relationship reinforces those expectations or redefines them through interaction (Littlejohn 2002: 235). The transfer of information that occurs through family and friends always is in a cultural context. Social norms set guidelines for both family and friend relationships and the communication styles that govern both.

You already know that because sometimes the way you relate to family is more likely to be predictable even though it changes as you mature. On the other hand, your communication with friends is often quite different from that with your family and much more subject to change as the relationship adjusts to interactions. You already know this too from having some sort of misunderstanding with a friend so that even when the damage to the relationship is repaired, it affects your future expectations with that person.

In a family setting, a hierarchy is set usually by the culture and its expectations. The strain of changes in family expectations as you mature calls for adjustment, not always an easy one. Relationships with friends, such as neighbors and co-workers, changes too with changes in situation. A colleague at work may be promoted to a position that changes your formal relationship and may have an impact on your interpersonal interaction. Relationships with friends may differ on perceptions of status as equal or not. You are likely to be more comfortable

Figure 1.1   A Filipino working the fields keeps in touch by cell phone.
Source: USAID/PHILIPPINES.

with friends who share the same social and economic status, but what really matters is a sharing of the same values and mindset. You may be in a social organization whose members represent different mindsets from yours, but you learn to accommodate those and retain the friendship because of your ongoing interaction. On the other hand, there is always some caution in your interaction to avoid offense that damages the relationship. You instinctively look for friendships that allow you to "be yourself," and not be rejected.

All of these relationships, though, give you insight into the ways others think, even when you don't agree. The information you get from such sources has credibility for you because of the level of trust that is a part of the interpersonal relationship. You may not agree, but you know, from the relationship, the source of their beliefs and behaviors. A friend might say, "Well, I don't agree with Luci, but I know where she's coming from." Relationships always are adjusting and changing, but familiarity provides expectations that validate information from these sources, even if that validation is conditional. The broader the range of your friendships and familial experiences, the better prepared you are to anticipate and understand cultural differences.

Extrapersonal relationships, usually public ones

These depend upon your own expectations and experiences plus communication from family and friends that conveys their experiences, values, and beliefs. A friend who called the emergency number 911 after stopping on the freeway to report a serious accident said he was amazed at how prompt the response was from police, fire, and ambulance. "Not much over five minutes for all three," he said with some amazement. That certainly raises expectations! On the other hand, personal experiences from promises about trash pickup may cause you to throw away brochures from the city assuring cooperation. Cultural experiences are telling too. A student called to say he had been arrested. For what? DWB, he said, translated: Driving While Black. The profiling of some police departments you may hear about is instantly validated by the experience of someone you trust. So, whatever is said in public channels that promises lack of discrimination on the part of that police department is treated with suspicion if not discounted outright.

In another country, trust of public communication channels may be an interesting learning experience. To avoid it being an unpleasant one, most people going to another country for a visit or to live, try to find out what public channels have to say, from that country and from their own country. Often, the cautious traveler tries to follow that up by talking with someone who has been there recently, or is a citizen of that country.

Our personal and public sources of information often offer us conflicting information that provokes critical examination. Strangely enough, that isn't always the case with systems of communication because we decide, often uncritically, which ones we will trust and which ones we won't.

Systems of Communication

Information is delivered through two main systems of communication: mass media and organizational media. Mass media include newspapers, magazines, radio, television and the Internet. Among sources available on the Internet are some of the organizational information channels for both profit and nonprofit organizations – their websites and chat rooms. In the mass communication channel of the Internet, these institutional sites co-exist but are distinctive from general news sites like those maintained by publications, broadcast networks and distribution channels like wire services, such as the Associated Press.

Organizational sites include those for commercial organizations, like Nokia, and nonprofit organizations, like the American Cancer Society. Organizations use other channels also to communicate with their customers/members, investors/ donors and such. Some organizational media, such as newsletters, appear as publications but often are available to subscribers or members electronically, on the Internet.

Organizations also maintain their own systems, called intranets, for internal communication. Intranets for multinational organizations may offer language choices to their global locations.

Global media systems, mass and specialized, have changed the delivery of information so that audiences around the world have access to commercial and noncommercial messages in a free-flowing manner (Newsom 2004a: 93). This is occurring at a time when originators of those messages usually are designing them for particular audiences. Global recipients, though, get these messages and images without the cultural context or experience in which to interpret them as intended (Newsom 2004a: 94). Another unintended consequence of global-ization of media is the spread of values, not always welcomed by some cultures and/or governments (Merrill 2004: 25–6).

Mass communication

Channels of mass communication include both local and international editions of newspapers and magazines. The international editions are designed for

---

Box 1.1 News sources and trust

Discussion questions in an online course that had participants from all over the world reflected considerably different responses to "What channel of communication about world events is most credible to you?" Students who had the most experience living or traveling in countries outside of the one in which they were citizens had friends with whom they had maintained contact, usually by email, and those were their most credible sources. However, students, primarily those in the USA, said they relied on tele-vision as their most credible source. This could be an interesting avenue for research.

Figure 1.2   Radio Africa interviews a young woman.
Source: Food and Agricultural Organization of the United Nations.

different regions, such as the Asian edition, or the European edition, and generally are published in English. The style of English depends on the origin, generally UK or USA. Some truly international newspapers exist, such as the *International Herald Tribune*, the *Economist* and, to some extent, the *Wall Street Journal*. Although readership of the physical papers is down, globally, Internet readership is up. Newspapers all over the world are finding the tabloid size, rather than the broadsheet, more acceptable, especially for commuters.

Magazines have suffered readership losses too, but Borders Books' founder Louis Borders launched a website that makes 150 magazines available on the Internet for a monthly fee. US news magazines most likely to be found in newsstands globally are *Time* and *Newsweek*. This calls attention to ownership of these publications. Media industries are now some of the largest multinationals in the world and include such giants as News Corporation, Bertelsman, Disney, and Time Warner.

Telecommunication industries are included in these media conglomerates, so owners, such as Rupert Murdoch, own print and broadcast media around the world. The BBC and CNN are internationally recognized broadcast systems. Communication satellites have made global broadcasting and printing possible.

Newsgathering and distribution channels are global as well, and their names are easily recognized. Two of the best known probably are the Associated Press and Reuters, although many countries also have impressive networks, among them the Scandinavian news agencies. Some news agencies are owned by governments that bear the considerable costs but also exert control over content. Global agencies tend to dominate as sources for both print and broadcast media.

Mass media content appears on the Internet in websites owned by these media conglomerates. Access is generally by subscription, although many offer a lead story and headlines to attract occasional reader/viewers who may eventually subscribe. Information at the global level through mass media is generally in English and is likely to convey Western values. Often this information conflicts with information available through national news channels, especially in countries where the government owns and operates the news media. An obvious problem for the print media is literacy.

Organizational: profit and nonprofit

Commercial companies use channels of communication to sell their products, either to retail customers or to other businesses. Companies include print materials, and, increasingly, information on CDs so that words, pictures and sound can be easily packaged. Magazines, newsletters and brochures offer other company channels of communication. Corporate websites on the Internet make possible direct sales and other contacts with the organization. For retail customers, chat rooms maintained by the company also make possible the sharing of experiences and information of customers or clients. Travelers can enter their comments about visits to places or travel on cruise ships. Music and book enthusiasts are also likely chat room participants. Younger Internet users are attracted to sites that support the popular culture.

Nonprofit sites are dominated by nongovernment organizations (NGOs), most of which are advocacy oriented. You can think of many, such as Oxfam and Greenpeace. Names also familiar to you might be quasi-governmental organizations, called GONGOs, such as two from the United Nations – the United Nations Children's Fund (UNICEF) and the World Bank. Volunteer nonprofit websites promote the organization's mission and also encourage contributions of time and money. Disasters in different parts of the world often elicit special appeals from relief groups. Although these organizations also produce publications, most of these are developed by representative groups, often local chapters, and are in the local languages. Literacy, though, remains a problem. Therefore, many organizations have videos in appropriate languages; however, unless these can be used by the local television stations, distribution is problematic. Nonprofit organizations are more successful at reaching people through radio, but again, this means working with local broadcasters. When media are owned by the government, the message and mission of the nonprofit group has to be acceptable to local media laws and standards. For example, a United Nations AIDS/HIV campaign urging the use of condoms is not going to appear in local media where any means of birth control is not allowed. AIDS/HIV prevention messages are not likely to be presented in governments that will not address the issue of drug use.

The limitations on information from all channels of information and the problems with cultural interpretation of messages is examined in the following chapter on concepts of the use of information for decision making.

Summary

You are living in a wired world where information reaches people in real time through interpersonal and public channels as well as through mass and specialized media. The Internet is a mix of all four, and is increasingly the channel of choice the world over. Limitations on the accessibility of information are the dominance of global corporations and government control. Technology, too, constricts access by the poor and the illiterate. With much of the origins of information being in the Western world, some recipients are likely to misinterpret messages – words, pictures and sound – because they lack a frame of reference for them.

Further reading

See T. L. Friedman (2005), Littlejohn (2002), McKenzie (2005), Merrill (2004), and Newsom (2004a).

Discussion questions

1 How do you get information about world events?
2 What sources of information do you trust? Why?
3 Can you describe the news process involved in international reporting for print, broadcast and the Internet?
4 Do you speak more than one language? If so, has that helped you understand another culture?
5 Have you lived in another country? If so, do you still have contacts there? Are they a reference for you to check information you hear about or from that country?
6 How do you use the Internet? How much of your time is spent finding out about international events? How do you go about that, if you do?

Research assignments

1 Find out how many students from other countries are attending your college/university. Look up the most current information you can find about each country these students represent: language used; religion(s) practiced; type of government; size of country; capital city; national leadership (title of top decision maker – could be a prime minister, for example, with a monarch as head of state); major source of income for nation, for individuals; major exports; level of education; type of news media. Prepare a brief summary to share with other class members.
2 Compare two countries that are democracies with the freedoms they allow their citizens to assemble, criticize their government, publicly share their opinions in speeches, publications, Internet, traditional media. What are the differences, similarities between the two countries? How have these and other democratically styled governments contributed to international public discourse on issues such as the environment, social issues such as minority rights or women's freedoms, and interlocking economic structures (foreign investments, for example).

Group discussions

1 Discover the cultural values of members of the class. Are there major differences or much commonality? How do cultural values shape exposure to information about controversial issues?

2 Can you think of a part of the USA in which you might feel uncomfortable due to a difference in cultural values? Have you had a "culture shock" moving to or visiting another part of the USA? What do you think caused the experience?

3 Is there another country where you think you would be comfortable living because of a similarity of cultural values? Explain.

4 What kind of media experiences have made you aware of a "shrink-wrapped world"?

Chapter 2

Concepts

Western democracy, including the key element of freedom of speech and of the press, is a product of the European revolution that was set off by the invention of printing with movable type in the late 1400s. The explosion of knowledge that followed, led to modern European languages, literacy, popular government, and newspapers. As governments and media develop the symbiotic relationship that continues today, governments tried to maintain control over information about their activities. Newspapers – and usually the public – wanted to know what governments were doing. The struggle between the two forces remains a part of the twenty-first century world. (Stevenson 2004: 66–7)

Objectives

- To understand how participatory government affects a nation's culture.
- To recognize the different interpretations of individual freedom of expression within cultural confines.
- To examine to what extent cultures encourage critical thinking and expression.
- To develop an awareness of tendencies to make assumptions about others based on perceived similarities.

Our view of the world and our role in it comes from concepts we hold, almost unconsciously, usually uncritically. Think for a moment about what information you feel that you need to know. Maybe you have a list of family and friends' birthdays to help you remember them. Perhaps you keep a schedule of things you have to do, either on paper or electronically so you can meet deadlines and fulfill obligations at work or school. Maybe you keep some information attached to your refrigerator, such as transportation or trash pickup schedules, perhaps school closings for weather. The information you accumulate and retain, in your head or physically, is all based on how you see your role among friends and family, at work or school and in the larger society. Although this is *real* to you, it is conceptual. Concepts are imagined and based on perceptions.

Your role, as you see it, comes from patterns you have observed in your culture, and largely rooted in your family experiences. As you mature, you become more observant of people you admire and may have many role models whose virtues you assimilate to make your own, framed by your own interests and talents. Culture is a significant part of this. Although culture is often defined many different ways, it is a pattern of behaviors rooted in values that are evidenced in the expressions of people. Concepts give you the guiding principles that affect your perception of events and people and provide you with a behavioral structure that governs the way you live. Over the years, experiences may change these concepts, affecting your behavior, even your lifestyle.

A graduate student in a culture quite different from his own lived the life of an ascetic for the two years of his master's work and the four of his doctorate. Outsiders would have thought he lived in abject poverty. His housing was barely adequate, his clothing bordering on ragged and his thin frame suggesting a minimal diet. After a position at a small university, lasting a couple of years, he moved on to a major university that compensated him well for his considerable research record and his excellent teaching. A man many thought would never change his lifestyle bought a condo, decorated it with expensive and tasteful furnishing, and, to the amazement of his friends who had never seen him alone with a woman, married an attractive, accomplished professional. What changed: his concept of his role. As a graduate student, he was focused on conserving resources to reach his goals. Once he achieved the status he had set for himself, he changed his concept of himself and thus his behavior.

While that might seem a rather expected behavior, consider some expatriates you may have encountered in your country or another. Their concepts of themselves and their role have changed because their cultural environment has changed. They, in a sense, live in two cultures – the one in which they were brought up and the one in which they now are living. There is another, more complex view of living in two cultures. That occurs when social, religious and/or cultural minorities must come to terms with the dominant culture in which they are living. Whatever the circumstances, the results are similar. A person has concepts that control behavior based on situations. Assumptions are made about how to act and dress in these two different roles. Because these roles are imagined, and based on interpretations, the flow between the two roles is seldom a conscious act. We "know" how to dress and act in each role and behave accordingly. An international student talked about going home for family occasions and adjusting rather quickly to a closer space between herself and others, but less touching, especially between genders. Her expectations and experience prepared her for the role change. An officer in a transnational company who was sent abroad to one of the affiliates for two years expressed appreciation for the coaching he got from colleagues who helped him put his observations and perceptions of the cultures he experienced into perspective. Two aspects of conceptual thinking are firmly rooted in culture: information we use for making individual decisions and information we use for making communal decisions.

Information for Individual Decision Making

Culture affects how much information we think we need to make as individuals. Think of culture for a moment in its micro aspects. Schools you have attended each had a culture. In a school where students wear uniforms, decisions about what to put on each day are limited. Even at the university level, if you are in a school where clothing is prescribed, such as schools with military units, you dress according to the role expected that day. Students who combine jobs with college classes wear their business dress to class because they are going back and forth from job to campus. Professors sometimes have difficulty recognizing students on weekends when parents are visiting. The role has shifted because expectations have changed.

Expectations of dress and other behaviors are part of the concepts we hold. The freer people are to make their own decisions about what to wear and how to behave, the more information is sought. We may want to be fashion pacesetters and start a trend others may follow. A major restriction is the acceptance of individualism by the culture. Another is the value systems endorsed by the culture, often affected by class or status. An international student commenting on her parents' recent move to Malaysia laughingly said that her mother told her not to show up at the new address with the décolleté she was wearing then at their home in Mexico and had on at a USA university when she was telling about the warning.

Often attempts are made to change concepts in order to change society. Efforts to give equality in gender are not restricted to a single nation. The efforts are worldwide, and not just through women's organizations. The United Nations has made an effort to give poor women in undeveloped countries a way to make money to give them an opportunity for economic independence, largely to change the balance of power in paternalistic societies. Sometimes the nation decides on its own to intervene. In Barcelona, Spain, an inventor, Pep Torres, is on a campaign of his own to get men to assume more responsibility for housework.

First he invented an ironing board that has weights to tempt fitness-conscious men to iron their own shirts, and then he invented a washing machine that operates on the recognition of fingerprints. If the prints don't alternate from wash to wash between those of the man and woman in the family, the machine won't work. Other efforts to change the image of male chauvinism in Spain include those of Prime Minister José Luis Rodríguez Zapaptero who got through Parliament fifty changes to improve women's rights, and called attention to these through an advertising campaign. He also created an agency to promote equality of gender in hiring for all branches of government (K. Johnson 2005). In India, several different regimes have tried to change the idea of female children being a liability and make them viewed as an asset to be treasured, educated, and nourished, both physically and mentally. These efforts include in Tamil Nadu a trust to help educate women, something being considered at the national level. The effort is to reduce the number of female fetuses that are aborted after a sonogram reveals gender, or the abandonment of female children that are born. The ongoing effort is supported by state-funded advertising and other promotional efforts.

What we need to know to function in a culture, a government and an economy is affected by the freedom of choice. When we live in a democracy with freedom of speech and right of assembly, we may protest decisions made by those in authority, on campus or off. There may be some civil restrictions on such protests such as blocking traffic, creating too much noise or impinging on the rights of others. But, protests are commonplace and expected. We see places of business with pickets. We get material tucked under the windshield wipers of our cars. Materials in the mail urge support for all sorts of issues.

To be informed, we find out about the issues and make our own decision about where we want to place our support in the marketplace of ideas. In a market economy, we expect to get what we think we paid for and are likely to return items that don't meet those expectations and demand a replacement or our money back. To choose what we want to buy or invest in, either in products, stocks or bonds or ideas, we have to gather information to make a good choice because this is an individual act.

You may know someone, or be that someone, who spends weeks deciding exactly what components you want in your computer. You go online to find out what is available and where. You read magazines, the editorial content and the ads. You visit electronic stores and talk with salespeople. Finally, when you know exactly what components you want, you go to a store, buy these and have your computer assembled. On the other hand, you may be someone who just wants a computer to do minimal tasks for you, such as deliver your email, help you keep up with grades or money matters on a spreadsheet and make it possible for you to prepare documents for you to retain in some reusable format and that your printer will produce on command. In that case, the information you need is limited to the functions of existing, but competing, products.

However, if you work in an office where the company is buying the equipment, the information you need is limited to making the equipment work for you and learning the software that may or may not be what you prefer. It could be that you may have had some say in what the organization selected. In that case, you were involved in our next consideration: communal decision making.

Information for Communal Decision Making

Although residents in democracies often consider themselves as more individualistic in their thinking and behavior, the whole political structure depends on their working together. Democracy is defined as free and equal representation of people in a government where every individual has the right to participate in governance. The difference is that the more open a democracy, and all are not the same, the more dependent these are on an informed electorate. In democracies, the electorate determines the leadership by voting for those who are expected to fulfill the ideas and policies projected in a competitive campaign for their jobs. In such a process, if those elected don't fulfill their promises or change course in unexpected ways, others, potential candidates for replacement, begin supporting different positions publicly so they can be chosen in the next election. The new candidates hope to replace those in office now perceived by the electorate as making decisions they don't like.

Governance of a different sort is represented in the way organizations are managed and how institutional authority is handled. Institutions such as profit making and nonprofit organizations are not democracies, although some may have varying degrees of democratic leadership. Nonprofit organizations are likely to be somewhat more responsive to their publics because they are usually heavily dependent on volunteers for support in terms of service and money. Companies that are publicly held are more likely to feel pressure from the marketplace, their shareholders and their regulators. Privately held companies, especially family-owned ones, tend to be autocratic. Information needs of employees vary accordingly. The freedom of expression within institutions and the authority to make decisions and take action is a part of the governance.

The structure creates a framework for the culture that is set by top leadership. The culture varies from one that is very open to information and one that is very restrictive, often called a "need to know" environment with information closely held. When top management makes all, or most, decisions, employees' information seeking has less to do with better ways to do their jobs than personal survival. Thus, institutions that need communal thinking often get less of it because of the paucity of information available.

Organizations that elicit ideas, including better ways to do things, and ones that reward individual as well as group efforts encourage the best kind of communal thinking. The same is true of political governments. The difficulties arise with two very human characteristics – sensitivity to criticism and resistance to change – both of which stifle creativity and innovation. There's no need to think individually or gather information about a better way to do something if leaderships won't listen, or worse, if punishment is likely to result.

Communal decision making in some governments affects the culture so dramatically that individuals limit their information gathering to very narrowly confined areas, usually on how to survive in the system. In some situations that depend on communal thinking, such as the military, law enforcement and firefighters, individual leadership is nevertheless encouraged. The histories of these organizations are full of examples of heroic efforts by individuals who took over in a crisis and gave their best effort, sometimes their lives, for the benefit of the community. The point is that individual thinking or communal thinking is not a given. Both are needed – communal thinking in an individualistic culture and individualistic thinking in a communal culture. At issue is critical thinking. Reasoned decisions have to be made given the cultural climate.

Thinking Differently and Avoiding Assumptions

Most cultures encourage what semanticist Milton Dawes (2004: 73) calls "Culturally-Expected Ways of Thinking (CEWT). People find the path to acceptance, and often success at the professional and social level, to be based on their acceptance of and behavior within the bounds of what is culturally accepted. How many times have you heard in a criticism of someone's behavior, "That's just not done here!" The "here" can be a place of business or a neighborhood, anywhere in the world.

CEWT, Dawes says, causes resistance to significant change, and he observes that with increasing accomplishments technologically, thinking too must evolve (Dawes 2004: 73). His concern is that we have to start thinking differently to meet the challenges of our shrinking but increasingly complex world. To do this means thinking in terms of the species, because technology is far ahead of revisions of

---

**Box 2.1 Assumptions signal errors in the making:
nationality ≠ religion**

In a class where a new professor from East India was being interviewed
by a group of students taking an introductory course, the result of assumptions made by the students was amusing, but very wrong. He was asked
about his favorite food in the USA, and he confessed to a preference for
Big Macs. Not one of the students had asked about his faith, so a number
of the students' stories marveled that a Hindu would be eating beef. Not
only was his faith Anglican, but also his father was a priest.

---

ideas, theories, and beliefs that need to be challenged to meet new realities (Dawes
2004: 74). The news headlines any day suggest that we seem to be creating more
problems than we are solving.

Part of the problem with technology is that we see each other, globally, on
an almost daily basis in the news. Uniqueness of attire and language has been
minimized, often due to a patina of internationalism or globalization induced
by technology. The result is we tend to make assumptions about others that
can cause difficulties. Students studying abroad are well aware of these hazards,
as are teachers who have taught in other cultures. We see people our age who
often look very much like us, even with a wide range of skin colors. They dress
very similarly, with some clothing adjusted for the climate. But, they are not
the same.

One public relations instructor working with his students from a US university and a group of students from Brazil engaged in a public relations project
for their client, soon found "I had two groups of young future professionals
at each other's throats over implementation because of cultural differences and
communication barriers." He said he had to intervene and make them aware
of their cultural differences so they could proceed, because they were not even
aware that they were "miscommunicating" (Melvin L. Sharpe, personal correspondence, February 7, 2005). Best to learn this before they are involved
in handling a campaign or other project for an international or multinational
client as public relations practitioners, each unit operating within a cultural
framework (CEWT) that restricts problem solving.

Miscommunication is often the result of expectations, based, of course, on
assumptions. One assumption is that English is always your version of English.
Wrong. Having taught in India and Singapore and England, this author can attest

---

to that, as can students from those locales studying in the USA. Even if the words are the same, and often they are not, the way they are used causes different responses.

For example, humor is almost always an issue, even without the need for translations – a fact that is almost instantly recognized by students from US universities who are studying in London. The advertising and public relations students at the London Centre for this author's university are puzzled by advertising that is amusing to Londoners, but not to them. It's not just the lack of a shared frame of reference. It's what is "funny" within a culture. Humor, jokes, and stories that have to be translated really suffer. So do analogies. A member of a team with this author in Hungary, where all communication in the workshops had to be translated, stopped the translator cold when he urged the workshop participants "Not to throw out the baby with the bathwater." Fortunately, the translator didn't even try to translate that to this all-male, middle-aged audience that probably never had an occasion to bathe a baby, much less throw out the bathwater.

Translations also mean that you have to speak much slower, to allow for the translation and for an absorption of the interpretation. When you speak another language, you also have to speak more slowly unless you are extremely fluent in the language and have recent experience in the culture. You may be saying something you didn't intend to say, but you can find out what the miscommunication might be if you have time to gauge a response. Languages are fluid; usage and meanings change. On a positive note, most people are willing to try to understand, and it is reaching that understanding that helps span our cultural frameworks.

Summary

Our culture gives us our view of the world and our role. Concepts we hold, almost unconsciously and usually uncritically, affect the way we think and thus the way we behave and communicate. We tend to follow paths based on acceptance of and behavior within the bounds of what is culturally suggested or even mandated. Learning to think critically, outside the bounds of our culture, is essential in a world where we have to work together for the benefit of the species. This line of thinking is a balance of taking individual responsibility while thinking collectively. To do so makes problem solving more probable because we avoid miscommunicating. Technology had created an aura of familiarity that is deceptive. Understanding differences helps to span cultural frameworks.

Further reading

For an overview of culture, go to www.wsu.edu:8001/vewsu/commons/topics/culture/culture-definition.html (accessed June 23, 2003).
See also Dawes (2004), K. Friedman (2005), and Nisbett (2003).

Discussion questions

1 Consider another country where English is used primarily, such as Singapore, England, India, Scotland, Canada, and Ireland. Can you list some English words or expressions that have different meanings in these countries?

2 Have you ever made some assumptions about an individual from another country that turned out to be erroneous? Give an example.

3 What other countries have you visited where something you expected wasn't there – transportation, food, clothing, religious practice, other?

4 Have you ever been visiting another country, or living there, and had someone identify your country of origin from their observation of you? What was that experience? Is it something you anticipated, or a surprise?

5 Have you ever experienced or learned of some law in another country that surprised you? What was it and why were you surprised?

6 What about a custom you experienced that you didn't expect?

Research assignments

1 Get information about values that are articulated by a faith different from your own. In what parts of the world would you expect to find that faith?

2 What country is the origin of some food products with which you are familiar, such as potatoes, corn, rice, bananas? How did those products become such staples in your own country?

Group discussions

1 How have global news media exposed you to different cultures? Give some examples of what you have learned from the globalization of news media.

2 What country's culture seems most alien to you, why?

3 What foods have introduced you to another culture?

Chapter 3

Politics

Knowledge of human nature is the beginning and end of political education. (Henry Brooks Adams, Chapter 12 in The Education of Henry Adams)

Objectives

- To understand how the political environment shapes behavior and thus influences the culture.
- To recognize the structure of different political systems and how these affect a nation's infrastructure.
- To identify governmental mechanisms for power sharing.
- To be aware of how governments liberate or constrain individuals' actions.

The impact of political structures on cultural communities can never be underestimated. With so much focus in the early part of the twenty-first century on religious-based conflicts, the degree to which faith affects the political climate would seem to underlie everything, including economic and social environments. Yet, faith is only a part of the equation. Political structure and individual freedoms are not always faith-imposed. The degree of transparency in government is often contingent on political processes that are part of the basic political organization.

Governments are historical systems of organizing a civilization. Most come from some sort of imposed structure from invaders and conquerors. If the intrusion was many years ago, the governments develop from the inside, as is the case with many Western nations except the emerging democracies of central Europe. Inside development also is the historical pattern for most countries on the American continent – Canada, north, central and south American nations. Few Asian nations have that history, although China, despite its many transformations, largely has controlled its own political structures. The emerging patterns are a global crazy quilt of different political structures.

Government Structure

Governmental structure indicates who makes decisions and how. Often public discourse centers on whether countries are "democracies" or not. Democracy is not all that useful a term in discussing political structures because the idea of "self-governance" or "governance by all of the people" implied is interpreted in many different ways that adjusts the concept of democracy to culture and traditions.

An attempt to organize government structure usually centers on whether a government is a federal system, a monarchy or dependent in some way on another nation.

A *federal* system implies political subdivisions that are independent from the central administration. A *monarchy* usually means the chief-of-state inherits the title and holds it for life. But, that isn't always the case. The monarch's term could be elective, and it may be that the monarch reigns and rules or there may be limitations on the monarch's power.

Monarchies may be constitutional, as in the United Kingdom; a principality, such as Monaco, or co-principality, such as Andorra; an emirate, such as the United Arab Emirates; a kingdom, such as the Netherlands; a sheikdom; or a sultanate, such as Brunei. A federal system can include federal republics. A *republic* means that a state has elected leaders and is accountable to a central government. That is a unitary republic, but a republic could be a federal republic such as the USA, where power is divided as specified by a constitution and real power rests with the subdivision holding the power to change the constitution. However, a judiciary that holds the power to interpret the constitution also wields considerable power in government. Then there is a people's republic, such as Communist China or Bangladesh; a socialist republic such as the unitary socialist republic of Cuba; or an Islamic republic structured around the Islamic faith, for example Iran. There are many other variations, for example military regimes, such as the Central African Republic; transitional governments, as in Afghanistan, and all sorts of dependencies from territories such as American Samoa to crown dependencies such as the UK's Isle of Man.

You have to keep up with the changes in control within governments too. A new leader is likely to make changes, some of which will have global consequences. The way the new leader came to power is even more important. If it is a military coup, then the country is likely to undergo some dramatic change, with restrictions being imposed on both citizens and visitors. If the change occurs when a religious group overthrows a government, federal or monarchy, the values of the faith, usually in their most extreme interpretation, are likely to be imposed. When a country is conquered or comes out from under political domination by another power, massive changes result. Even in nations where there is an electoral process, the outcome is not always predictable. Some elections may be contested and even if the proclaimed winner manages to stay in power, adversaries are often active in trying to change the situation, legally or illegally. Watch for change in troubled spots. Countries that already are in a state of transition provide ongoing uncertainty. In those nations, the power balance is usually precarious and the leadership difficult. News of change is just that, and whether good or bad depends on how new leadership charts a course for the ship of state.

Confused? Probably. Have a "so what" attitude? Careful with that. Government structures have consequences. If you are watching and listening on television or the Internet to news from a country, how you interpret the information depends on your understanding of that country's government.

You need to know whether government owns the news outlets, including the wire services; how that government interprets news; whether that government permits or restricts freedom of assembly; whether freedom of speech is guaranteed. You need to ask: How easy is it for reporters to get information from the government and how trustworthy is that information? How accessible are other people whose opinions are important? How free are those people to speak out, especially if their opinions differ from those of their government's leaders? Many governments interpret news only in the context of what advances the image of the nation. What is being reflected in reports from or about a country reveals only what is legally permitted to be collected and communicated. If you were there, you might discover that the reality many people living there are experiencing varies considerably from what is being reported.

Part of the equation is the level of education in the country, and who has schooling of any kind and how much? Who controls what is being taught, and to whom? Who is doing the teaching and how are the teachers being paid? What are the standards of living in the country and how good is the infrastructure? Are people isolated from each other except in the larger cities? Are they secure enough in basic needs such as food, clothing, housing, medical attention and personal safety to even be concerned about political matters? Even if they are, do they have some control over their lives, or do their governments hold all of the options?

**Box 3.1 How you say what you say:
WHO tailors campaigns for countries**

To see the impact of political systems and values, and to some extent also economics, look at the World Health Organization's effort to combat the spread of AIDS worldwide. You'll find that message statements needed to be adjusted to correspond with political rhetoric in various countries, especially Africa and India, and to deal with economic issues such as the cost of drugs for people who are HIV positive or have AIDS. Religion also is a significant influence, especially in countries where religion provides the political environment.

Institutional Freedoms

One clue to power sharing on the part of governments is the number of non-profit, nongovernmental organizations (NGOs) in a nation. While some nations have a number of government-supported organizations (GONGOs), it is the number of NGOs with grassroots support that is most indicative. Globalization has increased the proliferation of NGOs that used to be limited to international humanitarian groups like the Red Cross or international activists such as Green Peace. However, many countries now have their own "home-grown" NGOs.

Additionally, many nations have accepted United Nations or intergovernmental organizations such as the World Health Organization (WHO), the World Trade Organization (WTO), the United Nations Children's Fund (UNICEF), the United Nations Educational, Scientific and Cultural Organization (UNESCO), Universal Postal Union (UPU), International Civil Aviation Organization (ICAO) and so on. Opening up to these international intergovernmental organizations means sharing information, and the need for accuracy in such reporting has increased transparency.

Another indication of government power sharing, or the lack of it, is the amount of freedom granted transnational organizations within a nation's borders. Openness to Internet access and mobile phones is part of this, but one of the most obvious signs is the acceptance of publications and electronic media (including videotapes, DVDs, recorded books). Ironically, pirated versions of artistic materials sometimes are easier to get in restrictive governments than the legitimate product. With increased globalization of media has come some concern on the part of countries about the invasiveness of democracy. Right in

---

the middle of this are some international advocacy groups such as the World Association for Christian Communication (WACC). While the turmoil may seem disruptive, it has contributed to more global discourse.

Another sign of government power sharing is the freedom of commercial speech allowed. There is no universal agreement on how much freedom an organization has to speak for itself, either to promote its products and services or to defend itself when attacked. In the USA, commercial free speech is open to interpretation by the courts on a case-by-case basis. While some advertising and public relations practitioners have pushed for a broader interpretation to include institutions in the First Amendment, nothing is certain because there are no laws. In other parts of the world, commercial free speech does not exist at all, even as a consideration, and constraints on all private businesses are rigorous. Where the businesses are government owned, as they are in many nations, the power is clearly limited. Freedom to operate a private business is often not an option.

How people make a living in a country is not a matter of choice. It is a matter of opportunity. Government requirements for or restrictions on jobs proscribe living standards. We will explore this further in the chapter on economics. Nevertheless, it leads to our consideration here of individual freedoms implicit in or guaranteed by government structures.

Individual Freedoms

Students from the USA studying abroad in nations that seem to have similarities to theirs are often surprised to discover the First Amendment rights guaranteed to them, individually as well as collectively, by the Constitution are anything but universal. In discussions about solving communications problems at an academic conference, a UK citizen from London, England, reminded his conference constituents that there is no constitutionally guaranteed freedom of speech where he lives.

You also should know if you are going to another country, even as a tourist, what the judicial system is like. You don't have to do anything wrong yourself to get entangled with a nation's legal system. You can be a victim. Men and women students at a USA university in a women's studies class were horrified to learn from a guest speaker that in her country a woman who was raped was blamed and sentenced to death, even when the rapists had made it clear that their act was in retribution for something her brother did, an incident over which she had no control.

Judicial systems reflect a government's interpretation of the nation's values and the degree for government's need for control. When teaching in Singapore, students as well as colleagues reminded this author that the slightest negative comment could be interpreted as critical of that government and could result in being sent out of the country. For a citizen of the USA where complaining about the government loudly and publicly is a national pastime, it was a useful warning.

Singapore also has no right of assembly so there are all sorts of controls over presentations limiting "public" speeches. This seems almost ironic in a city-state that abounds in shopping malls and historically has been a significant trading center. The government's position is that in such a culturally diverse country, emotions could get out of hand in discussions of political, religious, and ethnic differences, so control over civic activity are necessary. However, in its gradual move toward more openness, a Speaker's Corner was opened in 2000, inspired by London's Hyde Park. But in Singapore, all of the speakers must be citizens who first must go to a police station with their passport or identity card and register their intent and their topic. Topics are limited, and religion is not one of them. The Maintenance of Religious Harmony Act has to be observed, as well as the Sedition Act and defamation laws plus the penal code.

Censorship of books, magazines, and newspapers is part of life in Singapore as it is in many countries. There the rationale is a conflict with Asian values. That is the same sort of complaint that is echoed in other nations that complain about "Westernization" influences in the global media. Some of the complaints are similar to what you are likely to hear in the USA, not "Westernization," of course, but explicit language, revealing costumes, and unacceptable behavior.

Government systems that try to protect their structures may intend to protect their citizens in doing so. Likely that is the case in Singapore where citizens often feel their government is a super nanny. However, the lack of transparency on the part of some governments is to hide activities that those in power wish to conceal from their citizens and certainly the rest of the world. US citizens have complained that since 9/11 (the September 11, 2001 terrorist attacks on the country), traditional transparency in their democracy has been compromised, many think unnecessarily.

International groups are active the world over in trying to improve transparency so that global public discourse is not distorted by unknown and unknowable facts. When governments are not forthcoming now in times of crisis, the global criticism often results in more, if only brief, openness. The USA with the torture of prisoners in Iraq, Russia with a sunken sub, Japan with a subway terrorism act, China with the SARS virus, and many other nations have aroused global criticism, even outrage on occasions, by not coming forward with facts. What some governments seem to have difficulty understanding is that transparency is a function of social responsibility. The more open a society, the more socially responsible it is to its own citizens and to the rest of the world.

Summary

Governments do seem to be loosening control on information about their nations (Stevenson 2004: 67, 81–2), perhaps because the global news media, especially the Internet, are so pervasive and attempts by governments to control news often become public embarrassments. On the other hand, with global media have come new controversies over the content of and control over global media (Grosswiler 2004: 113–15). To find out about governments, their organization, their services, their media and their citizens, you can find a number of sources on the Internet. However, one of the most respected and reliable is the Encyclopaedia Britannica's *Book of the Year*. How and when the information was collected is disclosed. You can get the form of a government, its internal organization, its leadership, its military, the demography of the country, educational level, health information, trade, media, transportation, and so on. Furthermore, you have access to comparative statistics, so you can look at one sector, such as government and internal organization, communication, language, religion, employment, and vital statistics about the population such as age, marriage, death. The comparative statistics help you understand the degree of control of each country's political system, and the resulting consequence of the degree of freedom for individuals in that system. Freedom for individuals can threaten governments, economies, and cultural social norms. However, with freedom comes individual responsibility, an ethical issue that will be considered in chapter 10 of part II. It helps to take a historical approach to the geopolitical scene according to Harvard University history professor Niall Ferguson, who compares the current era of globalization with what he calls "the original one," of about 1880 to 1914. Then global connections and faster modes of transportation were connecting the world economically, only to be interrupted by World War I (Sesit 2005: C12).

Further reading

See Encyclopaedia Britannica's *Book of the Year*, an annual publication and online. See also Ferguson and Mansbach (2004), I. Johnson (2005), Newsom (2004b), Schimmelfennig (2004), and Stevenson (2004).

Discussion questions

1 Have you ever traveled to another country where you were alerted by the US state department or a travel agent to some laws that you might not expect to be in place if you live in the USA? What were the laws? How did you feel about them?

2 The issue of global transparency is one that became a focus with print journalists, but has since spread to many other aspects of public discourse, including governments. What are some of the concerns here? Why does it matter, or does it? What effect has the Internet had on the transparency issue?

3 Can you think of some NGOs that have a global influence? What are their interests? Where are they based? What is the source of their funding? Who are their members, their audiences, what is their impact?

4 What impact does a government structure have on a national economy? Can you think of some examples where government affects not just the marketplace of ideas, but also the marketplace of goods and services?

5 Crises occur all over the world, some are acts of nature and some are caused by people. Does a government's structure suggest how effective one type of government or another might be in handling a crisis? If so, how, and if not, why not?

Research assignments

1 A friend you met in school has invited you to go home between academic semesters. "Home" is (choose one): the United Arab Emirates; Fiji Islands; Peru; Finland; South Africa. What would you want to know before you decide to go? Get the information. What additional information would you need after you decide to take the trip? What questions would you ask your friend?

2 You are writing a paper on university-level educational systems around the world. What types are there? What are the similarities to US colleges/universities? What are the differences? Would you know what to expect the background of a graduate might be from each type of institution?

3 In considering advanced degrees, such as a doctorate including professional schools in medicine or architecture, for example, what would be that person's preparation? (This is not necessarily an academic exercise. Many students who get their bachelor's degrees in the USA go abroad for advanced degrees. You might want to do just that and need to know what to expect.)

Group discussions

1 Compare individual freedoms in a country that has chosen one religion with another country, the government of which is secular, although most of the nationals belong to a particular religion. Examples might be: Saudi Arabia, Islam, with Turkey, secular although most of the people are Muslims; Bolivia, Roman Catholic, with Italy, secular although most of the people are Roman Catholic; Greece, Eastern Orthodox with Romania, secular, although most of the people are Eastern Orthodox; Thailand, Buddhist with Burma, secular although mostly Buddhists. Many other comparisons are possible, so you can explore.

2 Have you had an experience of attending a religious service in another country where that faith was the "state religion"? If it was the same basic faith as yours, what was different about the service from your experiences at home? If you were attending a service of a different faith from yours, what was the experience like for you?

3 Have you had any experiences in countries where the government has a Marxist base, such as Cuba, the People's Republic of China, Bangladesh? If so, what observations can you share about differences there? If you haven't had an experience in a communist country, what would you expect that would be different?

4 Health concerns affect all countries, and a government is always involved to some degree in getting healthcare to its citizens. Have you ever had an experience with a healthcare system in another country? What did you think about the care you were given? What about the costs? How did you feel about the medications you received? Does your experience influence your attitudes toward healthcare issues in the USA? If so, how?

Chapter 4

Economics

Economy is a distributive virtue, and consists not in saving but in selection. (Edmund Burke in Letter to a Noble Lord, *1796)*

Political institutions are a super-structure resting on an economic foundation. (Nikolai Lenin in The Three Sources and Three Constituent Parts of Marxism, *1913)*

Objectives

- To understand how economics expands or constrains choices.
- To realize the extent of the global marketplace and its significance.
- To develop an appreciation for the complexity of processes in a global economy.
- To appreciate the communication opportunities and challenges of a global marketplace.

Although many factors contribute to a national economy, the government is fundamental. Government structures and practices that cast government's role as controlling and distributing the wealth of the nation develop top-down devices for maintaining that control. Other government structures depend on the resources to run the national government coming from the nation's wealth in more of a bottom to the top system. The types of government, discussed in the previous chapter, provide some insight, but don't really predict how the economy functions. Major questions to ask when looking at a nation's economics are who makes the money and who spends it.

While that sounds simplistic, it really is very telling. If a nation's gross national product is substantial, but the per capita income for its citizens is low, that's a different picture. Citizens, who have little, spend little. The next question to ask is how basic needs are provided for a citizen – food, healthcare, shelter, clothing, education, and so on. If the government is generous in providing for these basic needs, then the system is such that although individuals may lack individual wealth, there is distribution of national wealth, controlled though it may be.

Such systems are often called socialistic, but few really are. The theory of socialism is that citizens control the production and distribution of wealth in a communitarian, rather than market economy. The concept is that the distribution is fair and equitable. Few nations truly lack an elite social level of people who are set apart because of their additional resources. A number of politically "democratic" systems tend to be socialistic in their economic practices. England is one of them, as are two of its former, now independent, colonies – Singapore and India. In all three there has been increasing privatization of previously government-run businesses, but government control of major resources remains.

So, the term "democracy" cannot be equated with the notion of a free market economy. All three nations would probably dispute this and claim they have a free market economy, but much is provided in all three by the government. One could argue that in the USA, the government provides many of the same sorts of protection: free education at lower levels, free healthcare to the disabled and destitute, and subsidized housing to some and some subsidized meals for children in school. However, the realities are quite different. In Singapore, private housing is costly and heavily taxed. So are cars, but mass transit is reliable and affordable. Government built and maintained apartments house most of the residents, but there are different levels of apartment buildings that reflect the educational and professional level of the occupants. Education at the college level is free. Food is inexpensive and abundant. Medical care is free to many and private medical care is some of the best in the world. Singaporeans complain, mildly, that the government is too much of a nanny, but the same government has been in power ever since the country was able to write its own constitution. It is likely to remain in power too because opposition parties are not treated gently.

India's government is much more reflective of the political party in power at any given time, and its politics are vibrant, although with so many parties coalitions are a necessity. Education, medicine and transportation are subsidized, but there are great gaps in wealth and ownership. It is not a good comparison because Singapore has about 3 million residents as a republic and India is the largest democracy in the world with a population that grows so much that any figure used here would be dated almost immediately. India's government in the last ten years or so has moved more toward a market economy, but still clings somewhat to its previous socialistic tendencies. England still clings to remnants of socialism. When the country began charging for colleges in 2004, there were cries of outrage. It is a member of the European Union, but not always with great enthusiasm. The UK has failed to adopt the euro as its currency and doesn't seem inclined to change. If you don't believe that, try to spend a euro there.

Nevertheless, London at this time, is the most expensive city in the world, having surpassed Tokyo in 2004. Why? Because the pound sterling is trading at about one to two US dollars, and more than holding its own against other major currencies.

Although only a few nations of the former collection of communist countries remain, two that stand out because of their contrasts are China and Cuba. While the size of the two flaws any serious economic comparison, the philosophies of both are rooted in Karl Marx's 1848 Communist Manifesto. Cuba, under Fidel Castro, has kept away a market economy and the island nation remains poor but faithful to its economic standard. China, on the other hand, retains the philosophy but under new leadership has reinterpreted its economy and aggressively embraced the market model, restricted, but flourishing so that the country is cited as being one of three world leaders: China, the USA and India.

In dramatic contrast, some nations of the world are still operating at the barter level, although they have a national currency, because of the lack of individually controlled resources. In many nations there is no middle class. In others the middle class is small and marginalized. Without a substantial middle class, countries are likely to be run by their elite who command top posts in government and commerce.

Understanding a nation's economy is critical to people working in public relations, marketing, advertising, and media. Educational and job opportunities, standards of living and the freedom to make economic decisions are indicative of people's freedom to choose. Sometimes it is easy to confuse cultural characteristics with the availability of choices. In some countries immigrants are the source of cheap labor because they are willing to take jobs that citizens disdain. The trade-off usually is freedom to make choices and to escape oppressive, even abusive, governments. The way governments treat immigrants and minorities in their countries is indicative of how economics impacts the social and thus the political structure. Both commercially based and government-based economies can be incentives for voluntary immigration.

Commercially Based Economies (Competitive)

Competition is the key to market economies, and thus the focus of most public relations, advertising, marketing, and media organizations. A global society has united markets so that investments, as well as products and services, are being promoted, advertised, and sold.

Financial organizations, banks, and investment companies are among the top globally in assets. Just as an example, in 2005, the top ten in the Forbes' list of

2000 leading companies in the world were Citigroup, Mizuho Financial, BNP Paribas, ING Group, JP Morgan Chase, Allianz Worldwide, Royal Bank of Scotland, UBS, Bank of American, HSBC Group, and right behind them were Mitsubishi Tokyo Financial, Deutsche Bank Group, and Barclays. Investors are shopping the world for stocks to buy, real estate to purchase, and companies to buy. The best Forbes 2000 stock market performers, over the short and long term included those in seven different countries. The one-year best performers Forbes named were Mittal Steel, Netherlands; KKPC-Korea Kumho (chemicals), South Korea; Orascom Telecom, Egypt; Hylsamex (materials), Mexico; Owens Corning (construction), USA. At the head of the best ten-year performers was Infosys Technologies (business services and supplies), India. The highest book value was British Sky Broadcasting, UK Media (DeCarlo 2005).

The USA's real estate market benefited from the lower dollar against other currencies, attracting individual as well as corporate investors. On the individual level tourism improved even though some visitors from other countries complained about security delays and other nuisances such as arriving at airports so early. Services, for example airline travel, got some stiff competition from luxury offerings such as those from Virgin Air and Singapore Air. Forbes also looked at productivity of employees and Greece hit the top of the list with the highest market value per employee in its hotels, restaurants, and leisure companies (DeCarlo 2005: 180).

Global markets have had other effects too on labor. In Japan, where loyalty to jobs was still part of tradition, in 2005 the former senior executive and vice president of NTT DoCoMo Inc., Japan's biggest cell phone carrier, left to be chief executive officer (CEO) of Vodafone Group plc's Japanese unit. The 58-year-old Shiro Tsuda's moved when he wasn't chosen as CEO of DoCoMo, a shock in Japan where loyalty to the company is usually put above personal ambitions. The *Nihon Keizal Shimbun*, Japan's largest economic daily, noted that it was "an unprecedented personnel change." The USA's *Wall Street Journal* called it "a major shift in Japan's corporate culture." And recruiters greeted the news enthusiastically, hopefully, saying it might set off a wave of top-level defections in Japan that would make it easier to get some top executive talent (Parker and Lublin 2004).

Outsourcing by US companies has made cities like Bangalore, India, a bustling market center, and created an interaction between employees of both nations that has involved exchanges and transfers. Although some US companies have recalled some of their outsourced jobs due to more available labor at home, expatriates from all over the world are experiencing living in other cultures at a time unprecedented in market development.

With more international experiences, companies now are more likely to adjust products to fit other cultures, at home and abroad. For some experienced companies such as Procter and Gamble, with a plethora of consumer products, adjustments have been common for years. For example, shampoos that carried the same name were modified for different hair textures. McDonald's has been modifying its menu for decades.

However, more changes are being made and planned to meet tastes and regulations. A *Wall Street Journal* story began:

> In Philadelphia, a serving of Philadelphia cream cheese contains 14% more calories than the same size serving in Milan. A jar of Hellmann's Real Mayonnaise purchased in London will have half the saturated fat of the Hellmann's Real Mayonnaise bought in Chicago. And a Kellogg's All-Bran bar bought in the U.S. has nearly three times the sodium as one sold across the border in Mexico. (Ball et al. 2004)

The ads may be similar and the packaging may appear to be the same until you look at the list of contents. Part of the change is due to demands from some countries abroad, like Japan, for healthier foods. Another part of the difference is due to both attitudes and laws. Europeans are very uncomfortable with genetically modified anything – foods or ingredients. EU rules call for identifying any

Figure 4.1 McDonald's ad on a Paris bus

genetic modifications on the label. Efforts by the World Health Organization (WHO) are another contributing factor. Although WHO only issued dietary guidelines, these were intended for government regulation and will certainly make consumers more aware of the nutritional value of products. What is especially interesting about product differentiation to meet preferences and laws is the retention of product identification to protect branding.

An observation by some colleagues who also have been teaching in London for the past ten years or so is that while it used to be so difficult to get a good cup of coffee that it was better to just order tea, this is no longer the case, thanks to Starbucks. The Seattle company has saturated London with its shops, and cultivated the tastes of Londoners to coffee, as well as becoming an oasis for coffee drinkers from other parts of the world. The product there seems to be the same as in the USA, but in London there appears to be more of an opportunity to buy Starbucks' coffees that come from smaller, ecologically sensitive growers.

Corporate products and services that are global in their origins, distribution, and consumption have, in many parts of the world, sidelined or put out of operation local businesses and industries that are unable to compete. It is some of these sorts of changes that the global marketplace is having on traditional ways of doing business that is provoking some resistance to globalization and "Westernization."

Government-based Economies (Supportive)

In government-based economies, most of the focus is on business-to-business (B2B) advertising, marketing and public relations, with government the major buyer. Transportation, technology, building, infrastructure support, and weapons are the principal sectors.

Box 4.1 An electronic marketplace: B2B wired connections

Both Mexico and China are using B2B websites very successfully. Mexico has nearly a fourth of all US cross-border B2B transactions, right behind Canada, and has increased its trade and investment with Europe. Improving its online approach has helped Mexico move beyond an earlier image of not being very businesslike.

B2B contact involves careful use of language, dates, weights and measures, and currencies. Language involves using one of about twenty commercial languages, and that means languages in which business is conducted. It is particularly important in dealing with government-based economies to offer information in a language with which the negotiators and buyers are comfortable. Using a familiar language builds trust because the buyer feels that there is a genuine understanding about the transaction. Those who can communicate effectively get the business. Literal translations simply don't work, so marketers must be sure the translation is an accurate interpretation of the content. In B2B transactions with a government, billions of dollars are involved but also the opportunity for a misunderstanding to cause an international incident of considerable consequence. (Chapter 6 deals more in depth with language use.)

Contracts with government have all sorts of opportunities for missteps. Weights and measures are one, and rather easy to monitor because these are fixed. Dates are another, and while these also are fixed although the way they are stated is not, you have to be careful about what calendar is being used. For example, some countries use an Islamic calendar. Just as a quick example, think of how often you date some correspondence with numbers: month, day, and year. You send 5/6/05 abroad, and only the 05 is clear. You could mean May 6, 2005 or you could mean June 5, 2005. Contract dates, as well as business correspondence dates, cannot be problematic.

B2B marketing, advertising, and public relations are much more challenging than their commercial corollaries because you must have a detailed knowledge of the business. Also B2B transactions not only involve more money, they also generally have more levels of approval, and this is why the language used must be appropriate, especially in nuance.

Much B2B communication is conducted online because it cuts the cost and exhaustion of trade shows and seminars, eliminates costly catalogs and other direct mail pieces that often don't reach their destinations at all, much less the decision maker. Also, online catalogs make it easier to update and to customize them for each business. Web seminars, generally limited to professionals, extranets, and the Internet, provide timely contact, although probably not any instant decision making. Government purchases are usually a much more involved process than exclusively commercial ones.

Part of that lengthy decision process is simply political and involves exhaustive processes. Another aspect is that a government, if it is acting responsibly, is making an investment on the part of all of its citizens. Therefore, government has a fiduciary responsibility that is much broader than that of any commercial decision where investors are the principal consideration, although manufacturers, suppliers, distributors and retailers certainly have an important stake also.

Box 4.2 Financial communications across the globe

United States
Regulators are stricter and investors are more sophisticated here than in overseas markets. The global center of the international financial media is firmly rooted in New York, so if your client can make it here, they can make it anywhere.

European Union
Issues involving European markets intertwine developments of the European Union and its 25 member states. The next challenge for financial communicators is the 2007–2013 EU budget, or "Financial Perspective," renegotiated every seven years. Many watchers anticipate key issues may drive a rift between governments and factions that could have broad consequences for the markets.

China
China's markets are growing faster than any others on the planet. Communicators have to penetrate heavy government involvement in the media, with many of the largest media organizations (CCTV, the People's Daily, and Xinhua) being actual agencies of the Chinese government. Still, there exists diversity of the media and fairly open discussion of certain issues, as long as they stay within the confines of the party line.

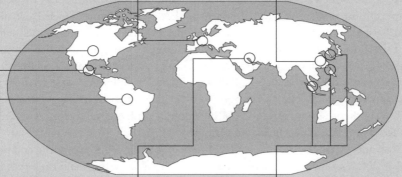

Latin America
With increasing competition and the rise of complex and sophisticated markets, this region is full of opportunity. Financial communications challenges now revolve around changes brought about by deregulation and more private-sector participation. Local markets also tend to interrelate by region, thus creating inter-regional markets with greater complexity and undefined rules.

Middle East and North Africa
Financial markets still struggle with political unrest, government interference, and stifling monetary/trade policies, while the reform needed to drive economic growth and foreign investment are being stunted. Instability and overbearing regimes threaten global-market integration, while spiraling oil prices and other trends hurt worldwide stock-market indices and consumer confidence.

East Asian Tigers
The East Asian Tigers encompass the economies and markets of Hong Kong, Singapore, South Korea and Taiwan. Communicators frequently cross these borders to provide support to global trade players, tapping the high growth rates and rapid industrialization that propelled the rise of this region onto the global scene between the early 1960s and 1990s.

Source: From PR Week: *Financial Communications Across the Globe.*

In a government-based economy, citizens have fewer choices. If they don't like or want what the government supplies, they have limited options. Only the very wealthy, usually a much smaller percent of the population than in market-based economies, have alternate avenues of supply. Another characteristic of government-based economies is a much tighter control over distribution of resources, who gets what, and how much. That control extends to how citizens are able to avail themselves of resources. This is not to imply that citizens are unhappy in a government-controlled economy. Often they feel that the government provides them with a safety net that market-based economies don't offer.

Summary

One of the best ways to compare political and economic influences on people is to examine persuasive campaigns, those that are government based and those that have a commercial economic base. Consider the effectiveness of such efforts and their impact on behavior. Although chapter 12 will go into more depth on this, begin to think about it now. You can look at internationally available products and services and recognize appeals adjusted to different value systems and see why some products are changed to meet the demands of consumers in different markets. (If you are in the USA, think of cars where steering is arranged to accommodate different traffic systems.)

Consider what choices are available to people in different economic and political structures, and how this interacts with their value systems and their mindset. When you are looking at ways of life in other parts of the world, look at levels of income and compare that with lifestyles. Economics is interwoven with politics, always.

Further reading

See De Beer and Merrill (2004), Merrill (1997), and Newsom (2007c).

Discussion questions

1 During 2005, a Chinese company (government owned) was going to buy a USA oil company and this stirred up much public discussion in the USA. How do you feel about foreign-owned companies buying US companies? Do

you know how many publishing houses and entertainment industries in the USA are foreign owned? Can you name some?

2 Can you think of an international campaign for a product or service that you have seen in the USA and then in another country that has made you aware of a different persuasive approach in selling the product or service? If so, what was different and why do you think it was changed for another country?

3 How much do you know about business-to-business economics (B2B)? Can you name some companies that don't sell directly to consumers? How do these affect the economy?

4 A big issue in the USA has been the ability of people in this country to buy pharmaceutical products from other countries and have them mailed to them here. What do you think about this? What are some issues you know have been raised?

5 One concern in global markets is how much one country subsidizes a particular industry that then competes in the international markets where some countries with the same products, often agricultural, feel disadvantaged. What are some of these issues?

Research assignments

1 Trace the global path of producing a single product, such as a car, to see why it is so difficult today to say where something is "made."

2 Look at the websites of two transnational or multinational publicly held companies to compare the boards of directors, their nationalities and background; the companies' mission statements and their policies on corporate social responsibility, environment, and employees. Look at their products or services and see where offices are located and who is in charge, as well as how much autonomy each unit has.

Group discussions

1 Choose a company you would want to work for that has locations around the world. What would you need to prepare if you were going to apply for a job there? How would you position yourself for employment in a company that might send you to any one of its offices?

2 Can you think of some products that you buy, and are available in many parts of the world, that are made by a family-owned and closely controlled company? What are the products? Who is the family? How much public information

is available about that company? How does this structure affect the company's public communication, responses to complaints, etc.?

3   What do you think about companies like Gap and Nike that have experienced some criticism for having "sweat shops" making their products in other countries? Does this affect the way you feel about the company? Does it influence your buying their products?

4   Do issues such as human rights violations keep you from buying products made in countries that have a history of suppression? If so, do you talk about it, or just avoid buying the products? If not, what do you think about when you buy the products, or don't you consider the issue at all?

Recap for Part I, Global Sources and Systems of Communication: Concepts, Economics, and Politics

Technology has the global society awash in information from satellite delivery systems, and this is layered on top of local sources, both mass and interpersonal. To even start making sense of such cacophony, it is necessary to organize the information into some meaningful context. Sorting out facts from opinion is a start, but even facts often conflict. Critical thinkers examine sources of information. Although the information may not originate with the source, it helps to examine two major sources – interpersonal channels and extrapersonal, or public channels. Public channels include mass media as well as corporate and nonprofit media.

What is communicated is intended for both individual and communal decision making. Some societies are more dependent on one than the other, but in either case, making some meaning of messages has to be done by individuals. It is how they act on it that is affected by their cultures. A major ingredient of information organization and retention is its usefulness, and economics is a significant factor. Economies are either commercially based, competitive, or government-based, supportive. An individual evaluating the significance of a message with economic consequences ranks it according to personal experiences with economic structure or structures. In a competitive marketplace, information about the economy is more likely to get more attention than in a government-based system where the individual is more protected from economic turbulence. Although this isn't always the case, because government stability and political structure also are factors. Government structures vary and within them individual freedoms and responsibilities.

Part II

The Cultural Context in which Information Is Received, Interpreted, and Understood

We can only interpret what we see, hear, and experience in terms of our own personal frame of reference. In our global community people are looking at the world through individual prisms. As public relations people, we recognize that in defining and describing our publics. But in PR practice what sorts of barriers does this create in complying with social responsibility? Social responsibility is based on ethical codes of behavior that have their roots in values.

Values come from learning and experience. We develop some values early from those who rear us, our schooling, our culture and our faith, or lack of a faith. We learn from experience what is acceptable in certain circumstances. Experiences force some accommodations. It is understanding some of these accommodations that this unit considers.

Observations are an important part of learning. Nonverbal interactions that come from action, sound, and silence are a part of what gets our attention. A friend's glance carries a message. The way someone dresses is a statement. Food and music are some of our first experiences with another culture. Because signs and language convey so much, we have to take an objective look at these before we examine some theories of symbolic interaction, the applications, and limitations. All of these are part of public discourse, so we must consider some theories of discourse, and, then, how we make sense of this by drawing some meanings from observations and experiences. We are truly a part of all we have met, and many of us experience living in two cultures on a daily basis, some of us only occasionally.

What is "right" in one set of values is "wrong" in another set, so ethical issues are predictable in a world of multiple "truths." Consequently, so are legal issues because these evolve from social restraints on behavior to preserve values for "civilized" behavior.

Advertising and public relations practitioners operating in an instant and global communication environment have to negotiate a mind-field, yes, not mine-field, but that too. Miscommunication at all levels, personal and public, has serious consequences.

An essential lesson in learning to be a global citizen is accepting the reality of multiple "truths," and remembering that there is no homogeneity in any nominative public. We may belong to something definable and describable, but we remain individuals inside of that "community," and never truly represent the whole. The last chapter in this part, "Developing a Worldview," from both a personal and professional perspective addresses the complexity of really being a global citizen.

Chapter 5

Nonverbal Interaction:
Action, Sound, and Silence

It is essential that we understand how other people read our behavior (not our words, but our behavior). (Hall 1959: x).

Objectives

■ To become aware of the "vocabulary" of the unspoken: action, sound, silence.
■ To increase understandings of differences in cultural context for understanding of time, space, social acceptance of sounds, smells, foods, touch, and physical adornment.
■ To build a better "vocabulary" for unspoken communication.
■ To develop an appreciation for and significance of what the differences in cultures convey.

Our behavior is often more telling than our words. Behavior reflects our choices, our culture, and our attitudes. Our gestures and our silences communicate, as do sounds, those we make and those that we find appealing. Music, dress, food, and nonverbal physical expressions convey meaning to others.

"We just don't have anything in common," a friend once said in commenting about a relationship. "He likes classical music and I like musicals. He asked me to go to the symphony with him, but when he said it was the classical and not the pop series, I was disappointed. What a miserable evening." That probably wasn't all due to the music, but it did set the expectations.

So does what we wear. A colleague commented on another's dress by saying, "She always looks like an unmade bed, and this is a professional setting. Looking that way is a sure sign that she'll never be promoted." Maybe, maybe not, depends on how she's evaluated by her superiors – by how she looks or what she does. You probably have heard this quote, though: "How you look speaks so loudly, I can't hear what you are saying."

Our first experience with another culture often is with food. A student, in telling me that her parents had just been transferred to Mexico, said that while home for Christmas she asked for chips and dip in a restaurant, much to the puzzlement of the owner. This was not in a "tourist" area of the country, and in this restaurant, there was no "Tex-Mex." She got introduced to what Mexicans call Mexican-food, traditionally more Spanish, although that varies throughout the country. Her expectations changed, and she was delighted with the cuisine she "discovered."

Although physical gestures and facial expressions might seem to be universal, since we are all human beings, these certainly are not. A smile has many nuances and conveys many meanings, some of them cultural. A direct look into someone else's eyes may not always be the intended connection from giver to receiver. Even silence communicates. You've probably had the feeling that it was not what someone said, but what wasn't said that "spoke" loudest.

Our experiences matched with our expectations and personal values often create our understanding of communication from another person.

Music

Ever have the experience of driving a friend's car, even briefly? When you turn the key, the radio comes on, and that's often music. What does that say to you? Maybe you smile, thinking that it's the same station your car's radio dial is turned to. Perhaps it is so different from what you imagine your friend would listen to, that you get a flash of insight, something you didn't know about your friend.

Another experience you've probably had is pulling up beside another car at a traffic signal and hearing that car's music, perhaps blaring. Maybe it's your favorite song and you smile and nod in shared recognition. Maybe not. Perhaps it's a sound that you associate with something you don't like. It's hard rock, really loud, and you like country-western. You look over at the driver, and think you know what you'll see. It's the sound itself that conjures up an image of the listener. For example, you hear mariachis and expect the driver to be Hispanic.

Our associations, drawn from our own values and our experiences, influence our expectations. Expectations frame our reception to communication. Music communicates and is symbolic. You hear a hymn and think of a religious sanctuary. You hear an aria and think of an opera hall. A marching band makes you think of a parade. Because of our exposure to different forms of music, we have a setting in mind, with imagined décor and participants.

Music has strong cultural ties, so much so that during World War II, the anti-German feeling in the USA was so intense that Wagner's music was seldom performed. Today rap music conjures up racial designations, as does "hip hop," although for both you probably can name performers of different races. The same is true of tejano music, although that is not limited to Hispanics. You can think of many other examples, especially the music for dances such as the polka, samba, tango etc. Music is said to be a universal language, yet often it retains cultural connotations. Recordings shared though the Internet are diminishing the cultural exclusivity of music that is more likely to be indicative of age groups than cultures.

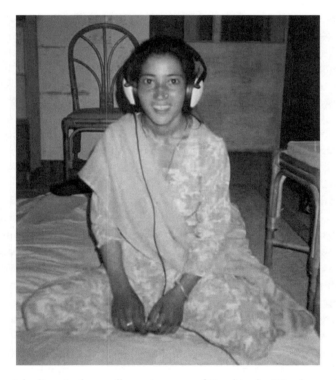

Figure 5.1 Asha lives in the small, tourist town of Kasol in the Himalayas of northern India. She is one of the only educated women in this region, whose society is one of longstanding patriarchal tradition. She has very little money, but with some financial support from her brother and friends in Denmark, she is currently pursing her dream of starting a children's school and computer center. As an educated woman in this isolated environment, Asha essentially is living in two cultures.
Source: Jesper Christensen www.meditation-inspiration.dk.

Dress

Choices of attire are tied less to cultures today with the ubiquity of Western styles, but you still have expectations of different costumes from some nations, such as those in African or Arab regions. What is more likely are some religious choices, especially head coverings. You can recognize an orthodox Jewish man, an Arab man, a Muslim woman by their head covering. You may see Indian women in saris, but probably not very young ones. The universal dress code for the world's youth seems to be jeans and tee-shirts.

However, it may not be what is worn as much as how it is worn that makes a cultural statement. A female student whose family recently moved to Peru was warned to leave at school some blouses that showed décolleté or be prepared to add a scarf because such attire would not be regarded positively. Changing accustomed attire to be more acceptable in a country one is visiting or living in temporarily communicates respect. You often are advised by travel agents or others to "cover up," especially if you are a woman. Men, too, get recommendations about the degree of "casual" dress accepted by other cultures. In some countries, it may even be a matter of law, not custom.

Both genders may find leaving shoes outside of a home where outdoor footwear is not acceptable can create a problem if the foot is otherwise uncovered. Hosts usually provide guests something for their feet, as do many public facilities that also don't allow outside footwear inside.

Yet another consideration is color. You may associate black with death if you are from a Western nation. For example, Westerners often wear black clothing to funerals. But in many Asian nations, white is associated with death. Purple is connected with death in some Latin countries and red in some African ones but may be even blasphemous in others (Ricks 2000: 32–3). The color of your attire is interpreted in the "language" of the culture you are in, not yours.

Violations of socially or culturally acceptable attire, even when tolerated, convey ignorance or eccentricity, if not arrogance. You've made a statement without saying a word.

Your body decorations also say something about you. Some are permanent, such as tattoos. Others, such as body piercings, are removable. Not only culture but age and social class often accompany acceptance of body decorations. While many equate body decorations with something as common as hairstyle, others do not, though hairstyles and colors communicate too. A woman with spiked hair of rainbow hues got on a London subway with a baby stroller and its occupant. No one said anything but the looks people gave each other were telling, as was the fact that no one in the car got up to give her a seat so she could hold the child. Another, more traditionally dressed woman with a baby had several surrender their seats, both men and women, when she had boarded. The contrast was interesting to watch in one of the world's largest and most diverse cities.

A student studying abroad one fall said she was dressing as plainly as possible, wearing no make-up and walking with her eyes on the walkway to avoid detection as an American in a country where US foreign policy had provoked a very anti-American attitude. Her nationality probably didn't escape detection, but her demeanor saved her from insult. Sensitivity to what you represent is part of finding your way in a shrinking world.

Food

Evidence of the "shrink" is especially apparent in our choice of foods. "What do you want for dinner," a friend asked, followed by "Cuban, Mexican, Lebanese, French, German, Italian, South Indian, Japanese, Chinese, or Thai?" These choices are available in the immediate neighborhood. We could have found Spanish, Brazilian, Ethiopian, Turkish, and Australian too, such is the blessing of living in a metropolitan area. Our appetites have become very sophisticated, even when the menus in the USA are not exactly what one might find in the cultures their names represent.

Our culinary experiences have cultivated an appetite for exploring other cultures, and we think we know something about them from getting a taste, experiencing the aroma of various dishes, all accompanied by suitable décor and some language samples.

By the same token, when US citizens travel abroad, they find familiar names, usually in fast food outlets: KFC, McDonald's, Wendy's, etc. The menus are not exactly the same there either. A KFC in Singapore has some items not likely on a USA menu, so does McDonald's. A manager for a McDonald's in Caracas said, "We can say that we always have clean restrooms and good coffee, wherever." So, why visit a dining place in another country that has food from your culture? It's a different experience. Try it. The differences are telling. In trying to figure out why the chicken in Singapore was cut into chucks that didn't coincide with US pieces, it finally became apparent that it is because the eating utensils were disposable chopsticks, although cutlery was available if needed.

What we experience with food is some insight into another culture. An Ethiopian restaurant in Washington, DC, has no dining utensils at all, because the expectation is that you'll use your hands. Arrangements in the restaurant provide for a quick wash with towels. Friends thought this might be amusing to watch on an initial visit, but if you've ever lived in India, you know the drill. There is a protocol for eating with your hands, although it is far less intimidating than working your way through a full Western table setting with an array of silverware, china, and glasses. An Austrian colleague once asked, quite confidentially, if other Americans dining with us would know what to use. Our "American" culture doesn't get very high marks in many parts of the world.

Expressions

Facial expressions and gestures vary across cultures, and an unconscious or automatic response can result in unfortunate miscommunication. If you are going abroad to study or on business, usually a protocol officer will give you some advice about unacceptable nonverbal communication specific to the culture you will be joining as a guest.

In the earlier reference to eating without utensils, in many parts of Asia that means only one hand, the right. The left hand is considered unclean for reasons that may become obvious to you when you step onto the hole in the floor – no flush toilets – and there is no paper but a bucket of water and a cloth for drying your hand. In a restaurant you will find accommodations for washing your hands before the meal in the room where the food is being served. In summoning an attendant to order your meal, you need to be careful because a curved finger or four fingers to beckon someone in the USA is interpreted differently in Korea and many other countries. If you are beckoning someone in Ethiopia, you need to put your palm down and repeatedly close the hand. In some countries, usually Asian, you may be seated on the floor for the meal; if so, be sure the soles of your feet are not outwards toward others. (Best to just tuck your feet under you and sit on them.)

When you were growing up, you probably were told it is rude to point. While that is often ignored in practice in the USA, it is considered very rude in Asia and Africa where it is more acceptable to make a fist and use your thumb to indicate something. Be careful with that thumb, though, an American "thumbs up," meaning okay is acceptable in many parts of the world; it isn't in the Middle East.

A simple nod of the head is not universal either. Nodding the head up and down in Bulgaria does not mean yes. In India a wagging of the head from side to side means yes, not no. For a no, you may get a finger wagging in front of your face in Ethiopia or a wave of the whole hand in front of the face in parts

---

Box 5.1 Crosswires in a wired world

The mix of language and social interaction (LSI) has its own identity that is attracting scholarship from many different disciplines, as you might imagine. Communication, which already draws from psychology and sociology, is joined by these two as well as linguistics and anthropology. Although the ethnography of communication has always been important to research in the field, technology's shrinking of the world has exposed us more to conflicts, especially across religious, ethnic, and racial boundaries. The internationalization of business demands understanding of power bases and structures.

Cultural traditions considerably complicate global politics. A wired world has put the spotlight on LSI.

---

of the Orient. A smile may be a polite way of saying no in parts of the Orient as well, instead of indicating pleasurable agreement.

Summary

Although one purpose of this book is to help you be a comfortable and knowledgeable global citizen, you are scholars too and need to know there are scholarly terms for these types of nonverbal interactions. The overall study of nonverbal communication is broader than this discussion and some additional areas will be addressed in chapter 6. Nonverbal communication as a field of study covers all messages people send to each other that do not require language: *physical appearance and dress* that often indicate religious affiliations; *kinesics* is use of body parts; *olfactics* covers smell, including body odors; *haptics* involves touch such as in a greeting, although some cultures, for example in India and Japan, do not touch in greeting; *proxemics* is use of space between people; *chronemics* is cultural concepts of time; *paralanguage* is a term used to describe the use of the voice including pitch, volume, pace, and rate (Neuliep 2003: 235–6).

Some of these need elaboration. Physical appearance and dress, body odors and greetings have not only cultural differences, but social status as well. A friend seen only in a sari almost went unrecognized on a flight from India to Frankfurt because she was in a business suit, wearing make-up, her hair loose and leaving a slight scent of very expensive perfume in her wake. In some cultures for some classes masking body odors is not appealing, an observation you'll make in some subways around the world.

Touching is very different for cultures, and for many religions. Even on crowded mass transportation traditional Muslims will make extraordinary efforts to avoid touching a member of the opposite gender who is not related. Standing close to people is not comfortable for most strangers in the USA, as any ride in a crowded elevator will tell you. However, at many social events in other parts of the world, the distance between you and someone you've just met may be inches, not feet. Backing away to get comfortable is likely to result in the other person's closing the gap for social comfort – theirs, not yours.

Cultural concepts of time are very important to understand if you have business appointments abroad or if you are invited to social events. In many cultures, you better be on time, precisely. In others if you show up at the appointed time, you may embarrass hosts who are not ready for you or spend a lot of time in a waiting room – hours, not minutes.

The nuances of speech include more than the choice of words, but also the tone and pitch at which these are delivered. That emphasis to the words has to be understood. Our global television delivery systems have injected some political host shows into other cultures resulting in some assumptions that our culture allows for rudeness, e.g. interrupting others; uncontrolled emotions, e.g. yelling; disrespect, e.g. embarrassing others by facial reactions to what is said. In many parts of the world, saving face is very important, and considered the only civilized approach to communication. Confrontation, as the body language on these shows clearly exhibits, is seen as rude. The pace and rate of speech varies across the world, and within regions, and that alone is just a pattern of delivery; but, combined with high pitch and unpleasant facial expressions carries a different message entirely, one of arrogance and disrespect.

Some understanding of others helps us, but understanding how others might interpret us does too (Burgoon and White 1997).

Further reading

See Neuliep (2003), Ricks (2000), and Samovar and Porter (2003).

Discussion questions

1 What does a person's choice of music say to you about that person?
2 What about a person's clothing?

3 How do you feel about your personal "space" and violations of it, including touching?
4 Can you remember your first experience with a food that is usually associated with another country, or perhaps even a different part of the USA? What was it? How did you react?
5 When you see produce that you don't readily recognize in a grocery store, are you curious, or do you just walk on?
6 Are you especially interested in the art of music generally associated with another country? What is it and with which country is it usually associated?

Research assignments

1 Find some research that details the different meanings for facial expressions to different cultures. Describe these and why you think these developed within that culture.
2 Look up research that explains what different gestures mean in different parts of the world.

Group discussions

1 As a group list all of the foods that are considered "specialties" in your region and why these might be unfamiliar to people in other parts of the world.
2 What foods do you consider "exotic" and discuss why you think so and whether or not you have ever tasted them.
3 Different beverages are enjoyed in different parts of the world – in spite of the ubiquity of Starbucks and Coca-Cola. Can you think of some you have had and enjoyed then not been able to find or replicate when you got home?
4 When you go to "unfamiliar territory," either in the USA or outside, do you make an effort to listen to the music that is connected to that region? Can you give some examples? Did the exposure cause you to look for more of the music to enjoy?

Chapter 6

Theories of Signs and Language

Nature speaks in symbols and in signs. (John Greenleaf Whittier in a letter to Charles Sumner)

Objectives

- To understand how some signs offer meaning in themselves and how others are used to explicate language.
- To increase sensitivity to the impact of the meaning of words to ourselves in using them and to others in hearing or reading them.
- To realize that message choice must be carefully made to insure understanding.
- To appreciate the subtlety of cultural implications in the choice of signs and words.

We gather meaning from signs such as gestures, as mentioned in chapter 5's discussion of expressions, as in pointing to indicate direction, beckoning or dismissing, greeting or expressing farewell. Public signs in international symbols let us know when to go or stop in traffic or crossing a busy street or watch for curves in the road, a winding pathway, where to buy food or fuel, find toilet facilities, put trash, or where not to use electronic equipment or cigarettes. We learn to recognize companies by their logos or trademarks, or signs for types of service – such as planes on highway signs directing us to an airport. Some of the earliest public signs were flags of different types, indicating warnings for storms, the origin and ownership of ships at sea or armies on the march. Other signs that developed early were symbols of faith. Among the earliest of signs were those used for advertising, so needed products and services could be found, such as bread and meat or medical practice. First there were just informational signs, but as competition for services and products developed, names or images were used with the product – a modern shorthand for these is the logo, which with a single image tells us what and who.

As language developed around sounds made to accompany gestures, so did a way of keeping records to aid recall. The British Museum developed an exhibit of such items that then became a book: *The Museum of the Mind: Art and Memory of World Cultures*. The Museum's Director, Neil MacGregor, said that a relationship between objects of art and production of memory is "tied up with some of the most crucial and definitive of human questions: a sense of being, issues of identity, of relationships and community, and of posterity" (Mack 2003: 7). The importance of memory pervades all cultures, and the items in this collection are signs and language. It is the visual, though, that often both inspires words and helps us retain them. Think of the imagery used in rhetoric to create a visual that inspires comprehension and aids memory.

Language is examined here in relationship to how signs relate to things – semantics; how signs relate to other signs – syntactics; and how codes are used in everyday life – pragramatics. Words themselves are symbols, which perhaps explains why the first efforts at representing language were to use symbols, usually an artistic representation, that communicated meaning but did not represent a word or sound. The early Mayan writings from about 650 BC were like this and have been called more of a universal system of traffic signs for the sprawling empire than a written language (Gugliotta 2002–3: 35). Other written forms of communication were also artistic ones but often representing a word or a particular collection of words that conveyed a meaning. The earliest written language that we know was also spoken is the now extinct Sanskrit of India. It was spoken in the fourth and fifth centuries BC and is the text for classical Indian literature and the Hindu religious texts. Greek is the most familiar ancient language because a modern version of it is still spoken today, and many of the ancient and classical eras of the language still exist. Although signs existed before language, they continue to be used because the image triggers memory, with all of its nuances (Jean 1998: 28).

Signs

Although words too are signs that stand for a meaning, *signs* as a word generally carries artistic, rather than linguistic meaning. As such, signs is an overarching term that incorporates gestures, the signs we make with our bodies; public information signs that we search for when we need directions; symbols that carry both the informational and emotional impact of gestures; logos that associate the origin with the goods and/or services available and also carry some personal reactions; and, finally, advertising, that brings us a direct and persuasive message encouraging us to think or do something.

Gestures

Living creatures of all kinds use signs. We learn the signs that help us anticipate behavior from nonhuman creatures we are likely to encounter, especially pets, ours and those belonging to others. If we may not be expected to recognize behavior, signs in public places often tell us that swans in a public pool may be aggressive or squirrels may bite and often we are instructed just "not to feed," for our safety and their health. Hunters learn the behaviors of their prey, so they can get an advantage. Body language is the most primitive communication, but is still in use because gestures can replace words, and when used by humans, may offer emphasis or empathy to words. Signs can replace words for people who are deaf and blind. Public accommodations in many places now require the use of these signs.

Public information signs

Distance communication signs were some of the first developed. Remember that before we began making signs, travelers used the constellations for navigation and employed some landmarks, although these were less reliable due to changes and errors of identification for mountain ranges, lakes, and rivers. The first signs made for public information were intended to help travelers, and we are still doing that. Sailors learned to look for lighthouses and, later, running lights on the craft themselves and, then flags. Semaphore signals are still used occasionally. Those traveling by land and by sea used maps, first crudely drawn before the art of cartography began. Signs we are most familiar with appear on products and in public places. The skull and crossbones that marked pirate ships still is used on product labels when the ingredients are as deadly as the pirate threats. In public places today travelers look to internationally recognized symbols for help: baggage pick-up, a suitcase; ground transportation, a bus and a car; steps for stairs; trash, a container with trash showing; female and male stick figures for toilets. We also get warnings: handcuffs; flames from a fire; items with a line drawn through them in red such as a knife or gun or lit cigarette. This is a modern version of the pictograph.

Symbols

While it might be argued that these pictographs also are symbols, when we think of symbols, we usually consider a deeper meaning than something just informational. Consider this definition for symbols: "The word symbol derives from the ancient Greek symbolon, a token composed of two halves, used to verify identity by matching one part to the other. It has come to mean a concrete sign or image that represents some other, more abstract thing or idea by convention, analogy or metaphor" (Jean 1998: 180).

Symbols often make us think of some sort of alliances, religious or political. Religious indicators are usually ancient in their origins. The Ichthus (Greek word for fish) is a symbol of Christianity first used in the three hundred or so years that the faith was an underground movement. It is an anagram for Jesus (Iota), Christ (Chi), Son of God (Theta Upsilon), Savior (Sigma). Certainly as familiar and much older is the Jewish Star of David. The six-pointed star is formed from two equilateral triangles. A crescent moon, an ancient symbol of the Sassanids, is now the symbol of Islam. Since the Arabs were the first to build an observatory (Baghdad, 820), many of the observances of their faith developed around astronomy. These three faiths share Abraham as a common descendent. In India, the Om is the most familiar symbol of this ancient faith. The symbol is made up of a representation of the three elements that characterize the faith. Om or Aum is a mantric word that embodies three sounds that represent Brahma, creation; Vishnu, preservation; Shiva, destruction. Today the most common symbol for Buddhism is a representation of the Buddha. The origin of the faith in India spread after converts abandoned India following conflict with Muslims and Hindus and left for other parts of the world where parallel schools of Buddhism developed with their own symbolisms. From philosophy we get the inner twined white and black portions of a circle with dots in the alternate color that designate Yin and Yang. Beyond the specific symbols associated with the faith, we also recognize the architecture of houses of the faiths as well as costumes and accouterments of believers.

Logos

Nonprofit and commercial groups both use logos for instant identification. Logos are the emblem of the organization, may or may not incorporate the name, but always use distinctive colors and art including type when it is used. Two activist organizations use either the full name, in distinctive type as in Greenpeace, or the initials in distinctive type as in PETA, People for the Ethical Treatment of

Figure 6.1 Religious symbols, nonprofit logos and persuasive posters, products as symbols. a) The Ichthus b) The Jewish Star of David c) James Montgomery Flagg. *I Want You for the U.S. Army.* Offset lithograph, 1917. d) The World Health Organization logo e) Yin and Yang.

Animals. The WHO uses a globe embraced by laurels with the medical sign for healing in the center. Your university also has a logo, probably the letters for the name, but displayed in specific graphics and colors. These are signatures, and the organizations have books dedicated to official presentation including who may use these and precisely how these may be used. Logos for commercial organizations also vary from the word Coca-Cola in its distinctive script to the sign of the stylized animal only for the Jaguar car, to simply an apple symbol for computer maker Macintosh, or the swoosh for Nike. The logo may have inspired the notion of "branding," from the marking of animals with a hot branding iron with a sign to indicate their owner when ranges in the USA were unfenced.

Advertising

Both nonprofit and commercial organizations use a combination of art and words to communicate. For nonprofit organizations, the time or space in media must be bought unless the media are controlled by the organization or commercial media can be persuaded to incorporate the ads as a public service. Newspapers and magazines usually limit such access to the back pages where they use these ads to fill unsold space. In broadcast media, time also is given when there is an unsold timeslot between programs. The unpredictability of public service time or space makes it difficult for nonprofit organizations to get out a timely message, so most depend on image or very basic informational advertising. Commercial organizations also use image advertising, often buying full pages that are not selling a product or service specifically but are selling standards of service such as quality and reliability. A good place to find these is in the *Wall Street Journal* because the intent there is to impress investors.

Signs as Persuasive Images

When you look at these signs, you have a reaction, usually both emotional and intellectual. The first response is intellectual because it is based on recognition, but with that comes memory, and that has an emotional component. Think first of the religious symbols. Your knowledge of, experience with, and attitude toward the faith itself determines your response.

That also may be true of some commercial symbols. If you like the product or have had good experience with the service, you may have a positive reaction. Some other attributes of these include style, so think about that when you see the golden arches of McDonald's or the familiar shape of a Coca-Cola bottle. If you are from the USA, both may give you a familiar and positive reaction, but in another country, these symbols have also attracted anti-American expressions, some violent, because the symbols go beyond representing a product and have come to symbolize the USA. You also may associate symbols positively or negatively with other countries. What do you think when you see a green three-leaf clover? The emerald isle of Ireland, probably. How about a sombrero? Most likely you think of Mexico. What about grass skirts? Hawaii. Lederhosen? Germany. Gondolas? Italy, probably specifically Venice. Many others, like the rising sun of Japan will come to mind.

It is what accompanies that recognition that matters. Do you want to find the product immediately? Go to the Internet and get the cheapest flight to that country? Or, is your response a negative one? If so, is it based on experience or only association with the symbol? You can see why organizations invest so much in persuading you to think positively about them.

Box 6.1 Thinking tricks

Our own minds often override our capacities for critical thinking, and much of this is cultural because it is value based. Consider this observation by Dr. Richard Paul and Dr. Linda Elder, writing in 2004 for The Foundation for Critical Thinking.

Truth and Deception in the Human Mind
  The human mind is a marvelous set of structures and systems. It is a center of consciousness and action. It forms a unique identity. It creates a view of the world. Rich experience emerges from its interactions with the world. It thinks. It feels. It wants. It apprehends truths and suppresses errors. It achieves insights and fabricates prejudices. Both useful truths and harmful misconceptions are its intermixed products. It can as easily believe what is false as what is true. . . . To exacerbate this problem, not only are humans instinctively self-deceptive, they are nationally sociocentric as well. Every culture and society sees itself as special and as justified in all of its basic beliefs and practices, in all its values and taboos. The arbitrary nature of its folkways is known to is anthropologists (if it has any), but not to its overwhelming majority.

Source: Richard Paul and Linda Elder, "Truth and Deception in the Human Mind", from *The Critical Thinker's Guide to Fallacies: The Art of Mental Trickery and Manipulation*. The Foundation for Critical Thinking, Dillon Beach, CA. www.criticalthinking.org

---

Language

The power of words is in their ability to frame our thinking. What we call something matters. Semantics is the science of considering how signs relate to things. A saying you'll hear from semanticists is "The map is not the territory." Reality is created by the meaning we attach to words, individually and collectively. The study of syntactics is how signs relate to other signs and considers the way we structure our language to create meaning. Grammar and punctuation give formal order to language so we can get shared meaning from unfamiliar content. The agreed upon organization of words with markings to indicate their relationship to each other is our guide to understanding documents like tax forms, for example. The common use of signs in discourse is called pragmatics and doesn't rely on the more universal shared meaning. Meanings are shared, but

Box 6.2 Misinterpretations = mistranslations = misunderstandings

On May 11, 2005 in Hong Kong at the China News Service, a reporter was filling in for her financially savvy colleagues and crafted a story about the potential impact of an appreciation of China's currency from a series of secondary sources. The story was picked up by China's *People's Daily*. That paper got it translated into English that converted the reporter's somewhat speculative language into more concrete terms. When financial news specialist Bloomberg's reporters spotted the story through its Internet software that sweeps for relevant information, Bloomberg sent the story around the world. With today's electronic interconnected news media, Guan Xiangdong's original story, now in somewhat garbled English, found its way into so many news outlets around the world that by the end of the day that one story had put the international money market traders into a panic and caused currencies to plunge, from the US dollar and the Singapore dollar, to the Indian rupee and the Japanese yen.

The currency market was already somewhat unstable due to the lost strength of the US dollar, against which the yuan is pegged. So when the story broke with the lead sentence that suggested that the yuan might be revalued or traded across a wider band, it hit currency dealers as a major change. Adding to the credibility was the fact that the *People's Daily* speaks for the Republic's government and had posted the story on its website. Furthermore the story's lead now said that the change would be announced after a scheduled meeting during the week with US and Chinese economic officials that did occur. Before moving the story on its wire, a Bloomberg's reporter had checked the story with the People's Bank of China whose officials refused to comment at that time, although denying the story later in the day. In the interim, about $2 billion was traded in just a few minutes after the Bloomberg story moved on the wire. Reuter's news service also contributed to the error by electronically sending the news that Bloomberg's story was quoting the *People's Daily* on the appreciation of the yuan.

Later in the day, the story got corrected when researchers for the chief China economist for the Standard Chartered Bank in Shanghai, Stephen Green, found the original story in Chinese and the English translation. Green's electronic note around the bank helped to adjust the story. The *Wall Street Journal* that reported on the confusion noted that it and its Dow Jones Wire did not pick up the Bloomberg story and never published a report of the so-called revaluation of the yuan.

Source: Andrew Browne, with contributions from Matt Pottinger and Qiu Haixu (Beijing) and James T. Areddy (Shanghai).*Wall Street Journal*, May 12, 2005, pp. A1, 8.

within groups, rather than among them. Because of this we try not to use slang or jargon in communicating across cultures because we risk misunderstandings (Littlejohn 2002: 57–8).

Semantics

You've probably had a friend say, in despair, "I just can't do anything right." A careful, and kindly, examination of what that means often narrows the "I am a failure" self-analysis to the more realistic "I failed a test yesterday, and had a misunderstanding with my best friend." That reframing of the situation makes it easier to deal with and corrects a negative self-image.

However, sometimes words are used to mislead and deceive. The English professor William Lutz has lectured and written extensively about what he calls "doublespeak" (Lutz 1996: 4). You've heard trash collectors called "sanitary engineers." Well, they are not engineers. The government speaks of casualties caused by "friendly fire." Not exactly friendly. Corporations refer to firing people as "downsizing." Sometimes the language is so opaque that the meaning is not clear. You'll sometimes hear this called bureaucratese or gobbledygook. Lutz (1996: 4) has said, "Doublespeak is incongruity, the incongruity between what is said or left unsaid and what really is."

Yet another example of misleading is propaganda. These ten uses of propaganda are persuasive devices used to sway opinions. Most of these are familiar:

- *Name-calling* can be positive – "a good student" or "a bad student" – but neither is informative and may not be accurate either.
- *Glittering generalities* are also uninformative. "Thousands of people came to free concert on the mall" may be exaggerated or understated. "You should have been there. Everybody came." Who is "everybody"?
- *Transfer* is what is supposed to happen when a celebrity is used in connection with an event or product; the prestige of the person is suppose to carry over to the less-known, probably new, product or event.
- *Testimonial* is a similar device but used when a celebrity actually endorses a product or service and claims to use it personally.
- *Plain-folks* is a favorite device of politicians who claim to be "just like" the people they are asking to vote for them, a highly unlikely proposition.
- *Bandwagon* is another device you hear often in an effort to get you to join the majority. "You need to come. Everybody will be there." "Why vote for her? You'll just lose your vote."
- *Card-stacking* is a common advertising device where you are told only one side of the story and relative facts are obscured or ignored. While we expect that

in advertising and can employ our own critical thinking before making a purchase, often in political rhetoric there is no opportunity to get "the other side."

- *Emotional stereotypes* are used to evoke all sorts of images, foreigner being one of them.
- *Illicit silence* is a subtle propaganda device like using innuendo or withholding information that could correct a false impression, like "Well, he's not from here." So?
- *Subversive rhetoric* discredits a person's motivation in order to discredit the idea, as in, "Of course she would suggest that, her family is heavily involved" (Newsom et al. 2007: 122–3).

When you experience these devices, you need to employ your critical thinking to investigate the intent of the message. What is it that someone wants you to think or do?

Syntactics

A sign that hangs prominently in a major newspaper says: "Write Like You Speak." That really doesn't happen, although newspapers do try to be conversational and write using words in a way that people ordinarily do, as opposed to the way words are used in, say a Living Will, or a contract. Legal forms use formal language and structure so that no one has to go into court to find out what was intended by what was written. We are more casual in our day-to-day use of the language, although we do count on grammar and punctuation as guideposts to meaning.

A Chinese graduate student got her professor to pick up Chinese newspapers in New York and San Francisco so she could compare the use of the language. She was writing a paper to see how Chinese was being used by expatriates. She discovered that newspapers on the West coast were using Chinese closer to the way it was being used in China, but the New York newspapers were using what she called "old style language," employing words that were not currently used in everyday speech in China, but still understood. Language is fluid. The grammar and punctuation keep it ordered enough for comprehension.

Pragramatics

What this Chinese student had discovered was that people using the language on different coasts were tied to their experiences that were not as fresh as the immigrants on the West coast who were likely in their first stop in the USA and not that far from their Mainland China experiences. Their use of words was

Box 6.3 Names matter

When Hurricane Katrina ravaged the Gulf Coast in 2005, damaging Alabama, Mississippi, and Louisiana, thousands of residents had to be relocated because their homes and businesses either were destroyed or so severely damaged that they had to be demolished. The term used in referring to these dislocated residents was "refugee." Technically, this is not a misuse of the word, but it had a demoralizing effect on people, many of whom were minorities and/or poor.

The slowness of response to their plight and initial inadequacy of the response had left them already depressed, and this term moved them to outrage. Some being interviewed on television about the situation in their area said, "And, don't call me a 'refugee.' I am an American citizen." Others were angered by the reference too.

David House, Ombudsman for the *Fort Worth Star-Telegram* in Texas wrote: "Expressions of shock and anger from offended readers, listeners and viewers presented the media with a mixed set of problems, including the need to decide whose side they would take in the matter – the dictionary or the people's." Readers told him, he wrote, that "Americans are not 'refugees' in their own country, especially when they are forced to flee a natural catastrophe."

He explained, "Those who are confused [about the use of the term] do not share the protestor's life experience as minorities who attack in varying degrees any form of insinuation that they are less than anyone else – one of the oldest prejudices they've fought and one of the deepest and most lingering wounds they long to see healed. The fight to preserve dignity is found among people from any group or sub-group. It's a pervasive conflict among humankind. Journalists who either forget or do not understand that probably need some exercises in reality."

He added that diversity is needed to help eliminate blind spots. Yes, that and some cultural awareness and sensitivity too.

Source: David House, "Reader Advocate, 'Refugee' vs. 'evacuee': The power of a single word," *Fort Worth Star-Telegram*, September 11, 2005, p. 5E. Reprint courtesy of the *Fort Worth Star-Telegram*.

different and certainly their expressions reflected the evolution of the language in its country of origin, while those on the East coast, as she observed, seemed linguistically "frozen" in earlier times.

Summary

The implications for culturally aware individuals is that when we get involved in translations, we want to be sure that our expressions are conveyed in the current codes for the language and that our word choice is timely and clear.

When students study abroad in a country that is using English, they often find to their dismay that the same word means different things. It takes a while for students studying in London to realize that putting their luggage in the "boot," does not mean cramming it into a shoe. A friend there is keeping a long list of words that are written the same way in American and British English, but not pronounced the same. Another problem in communication is adapting punctuation. Students using computers in the UK find their punctuation gets automatically "corrected" for them unless they put the computer into the "default" mode to get American punctuation.

A serious problem with translations is that these really can't be literal, and that is the major issue with computer-generated translations. Just to see how good these are, try to get an automatic translation in another language that you know and then get it translated back for you into English. It's amusing to try, but you don't want the consequences if you are trying to communicate with someone in another language. Really good translations are not that at all. These are interpretations. Sometimes there is no linguistic equivalent for a word or phrase, and you want the words and expressions used to convey the meaning accurately and to be current. A public relations practitioner who is a German national and also speaks and writes fluent French, Flemish, and English keeps his language skills updated by traveling because his clients who give him major projects to "translate," expect no problems with understanding and acceptance of their documents. An interesting activity you can engage in is to buy a product that is sold internationally and has several languages on the package. This doesn't have to be an exotic or expensive purchase. A paper tablecloth will do. You may find a package with 18 to 20 different languages. Choose two languages you know and read the descriptions for a comparison.

In communicating across borders another problem to consider is the concept of time. A friend offers a reminder in planning an event, "Remember, this will be on Mexican time." She doesn't mean time zones. Employee communications from multinational firms have to be sensitive to different cultural approaches to time and location. Much of this is directly related to the language because that is what creates meaning.

Further reading

See Chebel (2003), Jean (1998), LeGall (2003), Levenson (2000), Littlejohn (2002), Lutz (1996), Mack (2003), Newsom et al. (2007), and Ouaknin (2000).

Discussion questions

1   How many of you have had some experience with another language where signs represent words? What language? Can you give some examples?
2   Can you give some examples where a thoughtless choice of words created some misunderstandings? Can you think of some times when a national leader has used a word that had different connotations in other cultures that created some diplomatic difficulties?
3   Those of you who speak another language might offer an example or two of when you read something that obviously was a mistranslation resulting in something embarrassing or amusing.
4   Can you think of an example when fine art was used in advertising to convey a special appeal to a product or service? What did the art "say" that the ad didn't?

Research assignments

1   Find 25 examples of wordless signs that nevertheless convey cognitive meaning. Explain how meaning exists without words.
2   Find 25 English words that have different meanings in different cultures. Discuss how misunderstandings might occur in their use.

Group discussions

1   The members of each group can collectively create a list of "sayings" that are common to a number of cultures – human wisdom that has appeared in different parts of the world.

2 Develop in each group a list of words that exist in one language but for which there is no equivalent in another language because the experience in that culture is different.

3 Discuss how words have different meanings when the intonation or emphasis changes.

4 Share some amusing or embarrassing experiences resulting from miscommunication.

Chapter 7

Theories of Symbolic Interaction, Structuration, and Convergence

It is said that this manifesto is more than a theory, that it was an incitement. Every idea is an incitement. (Justice Oliver Wendell Holmes, Jr. in Gitlow v. New York *(1925) 268 U.S. 652, at 673)*

Objectives

- To become sensitive to observations that might be a source for the development of a new theory, the modification of an established one, or the reinforcement of an existing theory.
- To examine the underpinnings of actions and interactions of people with different backgrounds to see if a theory offers enlightenment, explanation, or insight.
- To analyze communication mishaps that might be predictable if theory were applied, thus avoidable in the future.
- To recognize patterns that suggest communication models.
- To gain understanding from the "storyline" or the approach taken by an individual in that person's telling of an experience or incident.

Communication models are constantly in revision, especially now that electronic communication is so ubiquitous and dynamic. Models evolve from theories that attempt to explain observations and assumptions to improve understanding and predictability.

Theories provide social paradigms through some assumptions or systems of beliefs. Although some theory building has begun in advertising and public relations, most of the theoretical underpinnings in both practice and education have come from sociology and psychology. *Structural functionalism*, with its origins in Plato and further development by Durkheim, Merton, and Parsons, suggests that a society's structure provides its stability, communication being a contributor to this social equilibrium. On the other hand, social change is said to follow natural laws, as Darwin and Spencer suggest, and that leaders need communication to make decisions. This is the *evolutionary* perspective, and another theory is that change occurs through *social conflict* as different social groups struggle over competing needs and goals, and names you'll recognize here are Hegel, Marx, and Engels. However, the theory frequently applied today is *symbolic interactionism*, with origins in the works of Charles Horton Cooley's study of the effects of environment over genes and Herbert Mead's study of the effect of language symbols in both individual and collective life.

Add to these sociological theories, some approaches from psychology that have been applied to communication. The effect of communication on the nerves and the brain take the *neurobiological* approach, gaining more emphasis today as technology has improved researchers' abilities to examine effects on the brain through computer compression. Also important is the *comparative* study of effects of communication on all living creatures. (Some of this has come from examination of post traumatic stress disorders – see Arbib 2005: 34–9; Bremner 2005: 27–9). Behavioral theories borrow somewhat from both but depend strongly on stimulus-response psychological studies. Yet another approach is the *psychoanalytic* that considers unconscious reactions, and the fifth is the *cognitive* that is concerned with what people do and with sensory input (Newsom et al. 2007: 116). That model, cognitive, inspired the very useful Ball-Rokeach value change theory applied often in politics and fund-raising. People are given a value test and compared with others like them or others they want to be like. They will change specific values they attest to holding in order to accommodate the values of others (Newsom et al. 2007: 116; see also DeFleur and Ball-Rokeach 1989: 29–43).

Symbolic interactionism – using the Mead approach of society, self, and mind – was expanded on by Herbert Blumer who used a more qualitative approach and involved participants with interviews, letters, diaries, life histories, and other autobiographical or self-reporting research. This came to be known as the Chicago School and emphasized the individual over society. A more quantitative approach, the Iowa School, was used by Manford Kuhn and Carl Couch. Since these early days, the theory today, as defined by Gary Fine and explained by Stephen Littlejohn, is: "the study of how groups coordinate their actions, how emotions are understood and controlled, how reality is constructed, how self is created, how large social structures get established and how public policy can be influenced" (Littlejohn 2002: 145).

Drawing from Shakespeare's observation that "All the world's a stage . . ." (*As You Like It*, Act II, scene 7, line 139), symbolic interactionism is expanded by Erving Goffman's assumption that any setting is a stage and people are actors trying to impress an audience (Littlejohn 2002: 145). Goffman says that people try to make sense of events in their lives by defining the situation. That definition has two parts, Goffman suggests: (1) a strip – sequence of events, the activity and then (2) a frame – the pattern that identifies and helps to categorize the situation. We can do this easily when it is a familiar situation, but it is the unfamiliar, something that you are doing for the first time that gives you some discomfort. Registering for a class is an activity that begins when you think about the courses you need, check the prerequisites, see if the course is offered the next semester, find out if the course is still open and then register. That is the strip and the frame is registering for a class. That's okay unless you are registering online at a new school and are not sure of the process, then you have to get some help. You communicate with someone, probably face to face, and in doing so give verbal and nonverbal symbols. You may display some anxiety or exasperation in not being able to figure out the registration process. In asking for help, you don't want to appear inept, so you are likely to project an image of yourself, even saying that while having experienced an online process before, you are just not familiar with this one. The image you project probably differs according to the audience, whether it is a staff person, a faculty adviser or another student. Your expectations of that person are different too, and it is the interaction that defines the situation. A staff person may be too busy to spend much time being sure you understand. A faculty member might tell you to get directions from the Registrar's page on the website. A student may be more sympathetic with your situation and go beyond directions, actually helping you with the process and explaining what to do when you register and a message comes back that the class filled while you were in the process of enrolling. First impressions do matter and encounters like these are the focus of symbolic interactionalism.

However, these microprocesses both affect and are affected by societal norms that are not that well explained by the basic theory. *Structuration theory* is an effort to explain this relationship and is generally attributed to Anthony Giddens who finds three dimensions to this social action: (1) interpretation/ understanding; (2) sense of propriety in the given situation, what is socially acceptable; and (3) sense of power, an outcome of accomplishing something (Littlejohn 2002: 152). Let's say that your university is supposed to be a welcoming place, but from your experience the only person who is helpful to someone "new" to the culture is another student. You've just experienced all three steps where the problem was interpreted as being your problem, not the university's and it is acceptable to leave you to your own devices to accomplish a necessary task or not. Complicate that by assuming that you are an international student and encountering many unfamiliar processes, and the student who agreed to help you is another international student because another student was "too busy"

Box 7.1 When the "same" language isn't

International students studying in the USA encounter some cultural differences even when English is a familiar language. Problems usually occur with social settings because social structures everywhere are fluid and interpreted subjectively.

After international students have learned to look for an apartment, not a "flat," and heard people refer to their "cell" (phone) not their "mobile," they still have to adjust to the local level of social familiarity. Some places in the USA, people smile and nod or say "hi" to total strangers, just to be friendly. In other parts of the country people pass without any apparent awareness of others. Students from countries where the social structure calls for reserve are discomfited, if not dismayed, by what they perceive to be excessive familiarity, when it's only polite friendliness or what would be defined locally as "good manners." If they are not responsive in that type of environment, they may be seen as "stand-offish," or worse, as arrogant. They may seek some explanations from other international students who have been in residence for a while so they can interpret their environment and adjust their behavior.

Another unfamiliar experience may be interacting with a member of the opposite sex. If a classmate they have been seeing and talking with in a class asks if they would "like to go out," they often have no idea what that means. They don't know how to respond to the invitation much less what to expect from such an encounter. Someone who says to them, by way of explanation, that the person is asking for a date, is no help either because the inquiry and the fruit by that name are a cognitive disconnect.

All of these rather common experiences are examples of symbolic interactionism where decisions are made on how to behave based on an interpretation of the situation, which is based on experience.

---

to help. What does all of that say about the culture of the school and the power structure? In public relations, a great deal of attention is paid to "reputation management," and these personal encounters (the micro level) contribute significantly to public perceptions of the organization (macro level). Where every person "counts" is imbedded in the corporate culture, the result is, generally, a better reputation.

Because your attitudes toward yourself and others are reflected in your language, think about how you would tell this story of your enrollment difficulties. If you are sharing the story with other international students, the rhetorical vision may be enhanced by others who will add their own experiences so that you come to have a shared reality. If you are telling it among a group of students where you are the only international one, some who are transfer students may share their stories, and make you feel that "your story" is shared by an even broader group of students. As such, it is a form of social bonding. On the other hand, imagine telling your story to some admissions counselors who encouraged your application. Would you change the story? Can you expect them to share your experience? Suppose they counter with an explanation that the first day of school is a stressful and busy time for everyone and that staff are often so overwhelmed that the "normal" friendliness and welcoming protocols are submerged. They have their own rhetorical vision that reflects their sense of reality. They might even tell you that the students who go with them on recruiting trips tell prospective students that everyone on campus is helpful and welcoming.

These vision stories are often used as efforts of persuasion, such as in a recruiting trip or a political speech. Basically, *symbolic convergence theory* is the narrative or storytelling act in communication (Littlejohn 2002: 157). It is used to tell stories that fall into three categories: one that is a moral tale, *righteous analogues*; another that is explaining how to relate to others, *social analogues*; and the third telling us how to accomplish something, *pragmatic analogues* (Littlejohn 2002: 158). Look at your enrollment story. You could tell it as a way you as a student intend to help others students, even seeking them out to give assistance. Or you could tell it from the role the student played in helping you as an example of how we all should relate to one another. Then, there is the simple "how to do it" process that you could put on your personal website to help others in the quandary you found yourself.

Application

You'll often find symbolic interaction used in all types of persuasive communication, especially advertising where the fantasy narratives of convergence attempt to get others to share the presented version of reality.

The sociocultural paradigm is a model often used in rationales for diversity in organizations, especially the mass media. The paradigm attempts to account for social and cultural variables that individuals can bring to interpret facts so that the information better represents reality. The question remains, of course, whose reality?

Limitation

A significant problem is the lack of measurement and predictability due not just to the number of variables, but also to the two major areas of influence: the individual and the group. Groups have little homogeneity internally because individuals exercise their own minds to make sense of the world, their world that is unlike someone else's. It is easier to find some commonality in organizations, especially small ones, and those that have some strong sense of shared values as in many nonprofit, activists groups. However, the larger the organization, the more diffused the culture and the more open it is to individual interpretation.

Yet another major flaw in applying the theory is the lack of agreement on the terms and their uses within the basic concept and the theories that have been spun off from it. Researchers have to confront both the qualitative and quantitative measures to establish meaningful results, and then have to confine application considerably.

Summary

The concept is so fragmented that generalization is difficult, yet it provides insights and instructive avenues for exploration. So far, it seems easier to apply to small groups than mass audiences. Nevertheless, the elements of symbols, language – both verbal and nonverbal – interaction, social objects, and perspectives all offer rich mining for understanding the consequences of global communications.

Further reading

See DeFleur and Ball-Rokeach (1989), Littlejohn (2002) and Newsom et al. (2007). See also *The Human Brain, Phi Kappa Phi Forum* (Arbib 2005) Vol. 85, No. 1.

Discussion questions

1   Have any of you ever studied in any school in another country? Where? How old were you? What do you remember about your experience that was pleasant, unpleasant? Why do you think you would categorize these experiences either positively or negatively?

2 In traveling in another country, have you ever watched, as an individual, groups of people from your country being "judged," either overtly by comments you hear or covertly, by interactions you observe? How did you feel about that? Did you feel that the "evaluations" were fair, based on the behavior of the group? Unfair? Why?

3 Have you experienced "value" clashes within your own culture? What are/ were they? How did you experience them: actions, arguments, what else?

Research assignments

1 Discover how many international students are on your campus and from what countries. How are they recruited, if they are, and if not, how do they "find" your school websites, alumni, relatives?

2 Choose two students from different countries to interview about their experiences with their US colleagues. What do their answers tell you about your classmates, the university's policies and practices? Anything you would change? If so, what and why? If not, why?

Group discussions

1 Consider how international students would view your school's "culture" based on (a) student activities; (b) student organizations; (c) living experiences on campus, off; (d) cultural events; (e) classroom interactions; (f) university regulations; (g) grading processes. Do these parts of their life on campus give them a positive or negative view of the university, the state, the nation? Why?

2 If you were to attend a university in another country, what would you want to know about the educational experience, the social experience, food, clothing, etc.?

3 Have you ever listened to someone relating an experience that you either shared or were aware of, that seemed, as you heard their version, that they were at another event entirely? What was it? How did their version differ from one you hold in your memory? Did their telling of the experience say something about them? What?

Chapter 8

Theories of Discourse

[Discourse is like] . . . a rich Persian carpet, the beautiful figures and patterns of which can be shown only by spreading and extending it out; when it is contracted and folded up, they are obscure and lost. (Plutarch's Lives, *Themistocles, also in* Apophthegms of Kings and Great Commanders, Themistocles)

Objectives

- To understand how what we know provides the background for interpreting and interacting with others.
- To realize how what we accept as "reality" is shaped by our exposure to information that comes to us "second hand" from mass media.
- To reach beyond our "comfort levels" in accessing information from other sources, other media and to follow how "agenda setting" in media influences public discourse.
- To search beyond what is said to understand the intended meaning in its context.

Agenda-setting theory is one of two primarily mass communication theories that considers the effects of mass communication that impact public discourse, what people think about and talk about. It falls in the broader category of effects of mass communication theories all of which refer to mediated communication, something that comes between the source and the receiver. The other is uses and gratifications theory of mass communication that examines choice of media. This theory attempts to explain why people choose certain media to gain access to information and how those various media fulfill personal needs and match personal values. We will not discuss this in depth in this chapter because of our consideration of public discourse, rather than choices of media.

The other theory that we'll consider in this chapter comes primarily from interpersonal communication. Speech-act theory connects what someone says with the anticipated reciprocal response that comes from expectations that respondent(s) will act on the information according to a set of rules that both parties understand. Integral to this, of course, is the respondents' understanding of the message in the same context as the originator of the message.

Two other theories that bear some mention before our fuller discussion of agenda-setting and speech-act theory are social learning theory and cultivation theory.

Cultivation theory also belongs to the mass communication effects collection of theories and attempts to explain whether or not exposure to information in the mass media, particularly television, is likely to influence audiences' perceptions of reality and subsequently influence how they interact with others. Most of the research on this has focused on the potential for violent behavior coming from over-exposure to violence acts through the mass media. Behavior is also a consideration in social-learning theory that counts on audiences paying close attention to messages and modeling their behavior based on what they remember, can act out and are motivated to carry out. Much of this research also has been grounded in the effects of exposure to violence in the mass media, primarily television, and many of the studies are centered on the impact of mass media on children. Because this chapter deals primarily with adult discourse, we'll just mention these for your information.

Agenda Setting on a Global Level

The notion that the mass media might suggest to people what is important to think about and talk about came to the late Bruce Westley but the primary researcher and developer of the theory is Max McCombs. Others who had similar ideas were Norton Long who, in 1958, expressed the idea that media suggest what people talk about and consider important matters of concern. A year later Kurt Lang and Gladys Engel Lang noted that the mass media call attention to political figures and issues that people should know about, consider and have some feelings about. McCombs' first study, with Donald Shaw appeared in 1972 in *Public Opinion Quarterly*. Their study looked at the 1968 presidential election with the idea that undecided voters might be those most affected by media coverage. Westley in 1976 posed the question of what makes the media agenda change. That idea was explored by the Langs when they returned to the agenda/public opinion investigation in 1983 in examining public opinion during the Watergate crisis, and they modified the study to agenda *building*. Another important step in the development of this theory came from L. H. Danielian and Stephen

D. Reese who noticed that coverage in a medium, especially a major one, can result in other media picking up the story. Their study, in 1989, was called inter-media agenda setting. They examined the *New York Times'* influence on other media especially on coverage of the drug issue in 1985–6 because although media coverage on the issue increased, the actual use of drugs in society had not. The most recent research, again by McCombs, is called the second-level-of-agenda-setting model. This model considers that an agenda is just an abstraction and many things other than issues could be on the list, many of them subissues such as tax reform under the issue of economics. The idea of personal attributes of political candidates, such as intelligence as a second level, came from research by Salma Ghanem and Dixie Evatt in 1995. (For a detailed history of the development of agenda-setting theory, see Chapter 11 of Severin and Tankard 2001.)

The result of all of the research on this theory has caused communication scholars to conclude that the effects of agenda setting cause audiences to consider what is covered by the mass media as significant and also suggests opinions they should hold as a result. The reason for these effects is that the news media function as gatekeepers, only letting through for public consideration and discourse what their editors consider newsworthy. Beyond that, the news media have the opportunity to show as much or as little of the information as they choose, like a photographer "frames" the picture in the viewfinder so the lens captures only what is "framed" for others to view. Of course there is another side to this, the audience. Some individuals may be more affected than others by the news depending on whether or not they see the information as relevant to them and whether the information offers more than they already know. This need for orientation explains why some people react more to news presentations than others (Dainton and Zelley 2005: 201).

As for the global reach of agenda setting, technology makes that possible with news on the Internet, satellite television, and digital publishing that makes delivery of publications available in different languages all over the world in the same time frame.

Proof of the impact of this was apparent in two major episodes. The most prominent was September 11, 2001 when audiences all over the world watched the four terrorist attacks in the USA and their reactions, some sympathetic and some joyous, conveyed around the world as well. A second example was the 2005 international Muslim community's reaction to a small article in *Newsweek Magazine* that appeared in all of its language editions, including the Arabic one, that reported, erroneously as it turned out, that copies of the Koran (or Qur'an) had been flushed down toilets at the Guantanamo Bay, Cuba, camp for political prisoners of the war on terror.

Another contributing factor is the growing number of ethnic media in the USA. New York city alone has more than 150 weekly and daily newspapers, and the Chinese language dailies in just that city have a circulation of more than half a million. These media pass along as well as report on occurrences in the USA and other parts of the world that are important to their constituents and in the language of their preferences. The emphasis is ethnic, and these affect the context in which ethnic communities place current events. With the connection of these communities to their homelands there is the opportunity for information to go back and forth. Additionally, correspondents are covering news in person all over the globe for newswire services. These stories are also framed by the correspondents and their editors (Feemster 2004: 4–5).

In considering what sort of items on a news agenda are likely to set off global responses, it is helpful to look at the five mechanisms that were suggested as early as 1973 as contributors to agenda setting as much as the actual flow of events (Funkhouser 1973: 533–8). What makes for news media coverage or non-coverage may be the following: adaptation of the media to a *stream of events* that create a pattern, and because of that may be covered because they appear to represent a "trend" or perhaps not covered because to report each incident would seem redundant; *over-reporting* of *unusual events* because of their sensationalism; *selective reporting* of some events not because the event itself is newsworthy, but some aspect of it may be, such as performers putting on a concert to raise food contributions for hunger in Africa; *event summaries* that show connections such as the impact of poor air quality in some developing countries where factories are polluting, or in some underdeveloped countries where unvented wood-burning fires inside homes are causing lung disease in children; *pseudo-events*, or the manufacturing of events, often for publicity, such as demonstrations or boycotts.

Media coverage is likely to set off reactions around the world resulting in dramatic public discourse that can affect both commerce and politics.

Speech-act Theory

This theory considers the use of language, speaking, as an act. The act has intent and anticipates a response based on a common understanding of the communication and a response behavior based on a commonly held set of expectations or rules. The response may be verbal only or behavioral, or both.

The speech act is said to have illocutionary force. Rules that govern responses may be regulative or constitutive. Regulative rules are those that are found in games. Chess is a universal game because the rules are commonly understood, but don't require speech. Poker or bridge, though not as universal, are understood because rules governing play that does involve speech are proscribed. However, there are different versions of these and the rules governing these versions are constituted by the rules. Constitutive rules create games and provide rules by which responses are expected to speech. There are four types of constitutive rules that tell you how to respond to a speech act: (1) the *propositional* rule, such as the expression of a promise; (2) the *preparatory* rule, which assumes the message recipients want the promise to be fulfilled; (3) the *sincerity* rule, which means that the speaker must really intend to do what is promised; and (4) the *essential* rule, which is that both parties must see this act as a contract. As you read or hear reports of international negotiations between the leaders of nations or their representatives, consider these speech acts. Think about the mutuality of the need to understand all of the attending rules when you hear or read commentary to the outcomes of such diplomatic or trade conversations. What you are likely to hear in the commentary is the degree of truth or the validity of the way the rules are used, and finally, the evaluation of felicity or the upholding of the contract. Discussions of nuclear proliferation, global warming, trade agreements, and such are loaded with such speech acts.

What you will hear in these discussions are five types of illocutionary acts: *assertives* that the speaker is speaking the truth in making a proposition; *directives* that ask respondents to do something; *commissives* that commit the speaker to future action; *expressives* that are the emotional side of the proposition; and finally, *declaration* that says simply because something is said it is so. The speaker

---

Box 8.1 Thought patterns and presentations

A master's degree candidate from China turned in the research chapter for his thesis to the committee. The content analysis was accurate, but the charts with his findings were puzzling to all three committee members until his thesis advisor spotted the problem and reversed the order of the charts, putting the far right column on the left. Since the student reads his native language from right to left, his thought processes work that way. His English-speaking committee members needed a more familiar arrangement. Discourse theory examines how we think, discuss and study issues. Difficulties arise because the rules of language set the pattern for how information is presented, and subsequently understood.

proposes to include all ingredients on packages for specific products as long as the respondent's country does the same and the speaker congratulates the respondent on arriving at this agreement that now is the new policy for both countries. (For a thorough discussion of this theory, see Littlejohn 2002: 77–80.)

The problem that occurs with the validity and felicity part of these may not depend as much on the intent of being sincere as the ability to fulfill the contract within the political and cultural environment of the parties. There is, too, room for all sorts of misunderstandings about the verbal meanings and interpretations of responses, as discussed in earlier chapters.

Summary

Global discourse is built on what is presented in the news media and what sort of conversations are held by political, religious, and commercial leaders as well as how these are reported – the act and the response. Much of what we know or think we know about topics in global discourse is seriously flawed, as these theories suggest.

Further reading

See Dainton and Zelley (2005), Littlejohn (2002), and Severin and Tankard (2001).

Discussion questions

1   Invite speakers from different religions to come to the class and talk about their faiths. An easy start is the three faiths that share Abraham: Jews, Christians, and Muslims. You probably can also find on campus or in the community knowledgeable people to talk about the Hindu and Buddhist faiths. Others may be available to you as well. What you talk about is how these faiths represent certain values that are held in common by their followers, although interpretation of that faith may have many different interpretations. (You don't have to look further than the many denominations in Christianity to see that.)

2   Look at some critics of the media to see what is being said about how events and personalities in the events are being represented. What do you think about the criticisms? Fair, not fair? Why?

Research assignments

1   Track four major stories in different media on just one day: a major metro-
    politan newspaper (or *USA Today*), a national network television newscast,
    a newscast by a national network radio affiliate. How similar are the stories?
    How different? Then go onto the Internet and see what alternative perspectives
    you might find – reactions from special interest groups or reactions by
    gender, race, religion, or ethnicity. What can you say about the "reality"
    of the four major events after such an examination?
2   Look up the major religious faiths in the world and write a brief summary
    of their foundings and beliefs. What does this suggest to you about how mem-
    bers of these faiths might consider world events currently in the news?

Group discussions

1   Different members of the group volunteer to listen to world news from other
    countries for a day to compare their treatment of stories with those in the
    US news media. Access to BBC World News is generally available through-
    out the USA. Also available are news media from Canada and Mexico. Other
    countries can be reached through Direct TV. Are story treatments on the same
    issues the same or different? Why?
2   What experiences have you had from reading local newspapers when you
    were living or traveling abroad? Did the approach to news seem to be the
    same? Different? How did content differ, if it did? What about pictures?
    Advertising?

Chapter 9

Frames of Reference

Oft expectation fails, and most oft there
Where it most promises
(*Shakespeare,* All's Well That Ends Well, *Act 2, Scene 1, Line 145*)

Objectives

- To realize the meanings that certain representations hold for us and be willing to put our judgments aside until our experiences are broader.
- To become aware of how assumptions we make about others and their circumstances are limited by our knowledge and experience.
- To recognize our own view of the world and examine it critically.
- To become sensitive to how living in two cultures affects expectations.

Our frames of reference result from learning, either through education or experience. Social status often is a determinant of which for any individual is a major source of knowledge. The higher the status within that culture, the more likely that individual is to be seen as "knowledgeable" about all topics, not just those in the person's area of expertise. There is some foundation for this because higher status individuals most likely have greater exposure to sources of information. Gaining knowledge exposes anyone to different perspectives and thus broadens frames of reference. Frames modify our assumptions.

Assumptions are a short-cut in thinking about our world, and, as mentioned in Chapter 8, the basis for our social reality.[1] The more informed we are, the closer our assumptions are to an objective perspective. A recent study of international

---

[1] See www.Irz-muenchen.de/~Prof.Helle/znaniecki1.htm (Florian Znaniecki). Znaniecki says there are four systems of social reality: social actions (primarily between two people), social relations, social persons, and social groups.

public relations educators suggested strong desires for more global knowledge, especially about Hispanic countries and Asia, particularly the Middle East, and also Africa. Responders wanted more training in communicating with and working within cultures.[2]

Communication is complicated enough even within cultures, a good example being the prevalence of racism.

A focus within the scientific community, as well as political and academic communities, is understanding racism, since it is a major cause for dissent. An assumption by many well-educated communities is that racism is inevitable. A study by a Canadian psychologist challenges that notion. Dr. William Cunningham of the University of Toronto says that an entirely emotional response, from the brain's amygdala, can be overridden by the cognitive areas of the pre-frontal cortex and the anterior cingulated cortex.

Psychologist Susan Fiske of Princeton University says that when someone is forced to look at a person as an individual, race-based stereotypes evaporate, and the good news is that we can control how we look at people because each of us is responsible for what we do with information to which we are exposed (Begley 2004: B1). Yet another study, this one examining cognitive cues from a Kenya television program with an integrative intent, suggested that social learning can occur (Amienyi 2004: 12–23).

Even in Africa, where there is primarily one race, there are difficulties with cultural integration. This is seen as a major block to national development because many undeveloped communities in some African nations have not been successful in gaining change-generating interactions to benefit improvement of their social systems that eliminates rebellions and stabilizes the country. The notion of using entertainment media for change is not new, as the traveling "theater" groups have demonstrated, especially in India.

Attachment of Meanings

Images we carry in our heads influence the meanings we attach to symbols that generate an immediate response. Consider four sources for symbols that stimulate a non-cognitive response: commercial logos or signs, costumes, belief-oriented representations, international organizations.

Commercial signs you might think of are the "golden arches" of McDonald's restaurants or the cursive script of Coca-Cola. These symbols not only are

---

[2] Survey by Dr. Mel Sharpe, International Section, Public Relations Society of America, June, 2005.

Figure 9.1 A British humorous billboard that probably would not be amusing to Americans.
Source: Maskim Noy, http://maxnoy.com

associated with the products, but also with the USA. In many parts of the world these commercial signs represent the USA as much as the nation's flag. Consider the Swiss army knife, distinctive and recognizable regardless of its size due to the cross with the circle. If you just saw that logo, would you think of the knife?

Costumes that may come to mind are sombreros, grass skirts, and leder-hosen. When you see a sombrero, do you think of somewhere in the southern part of the Americas, perhaps Mexico? Does the grass skirt make you think of Hawaii? What about lederhosen? Is it Germany or Switzerland you are seeing? Other symbols that indicate location are the Leprechaun (Ireland), or a gondola (Italy). You can think of many more. Beyond the location itself, what do you also associate with that part of the world?

Belief-oriented or religious symbols also inspire an emotional response. The sign of the Hindu Om stands for a mantric word interpreted as having three sounds representing Brahma or creation, Vishnu or preservation, and Siva or destruction, and consisting of the same three sounds representing waking, dreams, and deep sleep along with the following silence, which is fulfillment. Another sign that often appears on cars in the USA is the Ichthus, the word for fish in Greek, and thus a fish shape. For Christians, the word is an anagram: Jesus (Iota), Christ (Chi), Son of God (Theta Upsilon), Savior (Sigma). The symbol was used primarily in the three hundred years that Christianity was an underground movement. A six-pointed star formed by two equilateral triangles is recognized as the Star of David, the primary identification of the Jewish faith. The circle with a curved line through the middle and one side black and the other white represents the Yin and Yang of a philosophy endorsed by many Asian communities, but primarily the Chinese. Consider what associated thoughts you have when you see these symbols (see pp. 59–60).

International groups and politically persuasive symbols also generate a reaction, either supportive of the cause or critical of what the organization represents.

Box 9.1 News coverage and celebrity creations

What makes a "celebrity"? The culture, and only as long as there is active interest in that person, so "fame" is fleeting. There are sports celebrities, entertainment celebrities, political celebrities, social celebrities, and even "news" celebrities whose "fame" usually lasts only as long as media coverage is focused on that individual. Values change and the celebrity spotlight moves on.

This is not to minimize the impact of these "assigned" values to an individual. In 2005, the case of Terry Schiavo, who was hospitalized in what had been defined as a "vegetative" state, became the focus of international attention when, after ten years, her husband decided to have her feeding tube withdrawn so she could die peacefully. Her parents objected, saying her condition was reversible under the proper care. The governor of the state of Florida agreed and prevented the tube's removal until the courts made their decision.

The case drew the attention of the Vatican, organizations for the disabled, and all supporters of the right to life. The unaware woman never knew what social reality had been constructed by her condition – one that met all three steps in the process for the concept of world-maintenance of a socially constructed reality: socialization – interaction, communication and understanding; social control – government involvement and legal actions; legitimation – involving questions of theology and philosophy.

Consider what you think when you see PETA, People for the Ethical Treatment of Animals, or WHO, the World Health Organization or the cross of the American Red Cross, although associated organizations in other parts of the world use different symbols.

The way people dress or wear their hair also is a symbol of a lifestyle. The way we "decorate" ourselves either with clothing or body piercings or tattoos says something to beholders who will make assumptions about us.

If you go to websites for information, you are exposed to both information and image. An image is not an accurate representation, but a representation made "fuzzy" by your perception. Organizational websites are a persuasive tool and the generators of those messages want you to react positively. Most work hard not to violate any cultural taboos or offend any faith group.

Experience

Culture affects our values that have an impact on how we put experience into a context.

Most Western nations, despite their cultural difference, reflect the following values: individual sense of responsibility, respect for laws established through participatory systems, a value of time, practicality, expectation of cleanliness and order in public as well as private places, and a competitive nature with an emphasis on winning and aggressiveness.

Although the USA was influenced in its founding by primarily a Western culture, it is increasingly being influenced by an influx of both Asian and Hispanic immigrants. How that might change some typically US values remains to be seen. However, some values that set the USA apart from some other Western nations are some different values: problem-solving abilities – a "can do" attitude, creativity and originality, work ethic, volunteerism, trust, a faith-based culture with more "practicing" religious people of all faiths and a diversity of cultures. Some of this difference can be seen in a difference in the attitude toward freedom of speech. In the USA many "speech codes" have been struck down by the courts, especially some designated to stop "hate speech," because of the First Amendment. That freedom is unique to the USA, and the European Union's view of human rights does not include such freedom, nor do the laws of most of its member nations (Seligman 2005: 97–8).

A major influence, especially in some parts of the USA, comes from values reflected by Latin American cultures. Although these differ, some dramatically, there are some similarities. Consider the following: religious reference, respect for authority, celebration of those in power, paternalistic society. The consequences of these values include: acceptance bordering on fatalistic, suppressed hostility, acceptance of dominance as superiority and little support for the "underdog." Asian cultures are more likely to see Latin American cultures as aligned with the West due to the influence on them from Spain and Portugal and visualize themselves as quite different. However, some Latin American values, such as religious reference, usually Roman Catholic, and its paternalistic society create a view of the world that is often in conflict with Western societies, which having been democratic for centuries, often challenge those in authority because they assume that is a right of freedom.

As with most cultures, all Asian nations are not the same, but you are more likely to find consistency in value systems here despite the diversity of faiths and philosophies. Asian values include: regard for the community over the individual, respect for structure, importance of family unity, an ethical social system that defines unequal relationships due to economic or social class, concern for the here and now rather than an afterlife, creativity in art and invention, conservation of resources and an integration of symbols and images into everyday life. The effects of these are: a close-knit society not open to the integration of foreigners, a highly structured society with economic as well as social and cultural barriers, a traditional society in which the family is highly significant, a society in which the individual is less important than the group, a paternalistic society and an inventive and creative society that is resourceful.

As with most cultures, belief systems are very important to an Asian worldview. These Asian values are influenced by two philosophies and three major religions. China's philosophy, drawn particularly from the teachings of Lao Tzu and Confucius, is a significant influence. Lao Tzu's teachings, called Taoism, endorse a retreat from civilization to nature to attain harmony with Tao, the supreme governing force behind the universe. His contemporary, Confucius, had even greater influence to such an extent that many equate Asian values to Confucian values. Confucius was a teacher of ethics. His teachings included the unity of the family and a formal ethical system defining personal relationships as an ideal moral order. It was Confucian scholar Mencius who tied economics to ethics and was responsible for ideas regarding the conservation of natural resources.

In addition to philosophy, religion also is a major factor in Asian values. The oldest of the three major faiths is Hinduism, which teaches that reality is one: oneness of all things, of gods as well as living things. Of the two levels of worship, the philosophical and the devotional, it is the devotional that is more popular. The highest level is self-realization, which involves giving up a limited personality for an infinite one. The second oldest is Buddhism which is a system of human conduct with little basis in the supernatural. Its founder, Siddhartha Gautama, was born about 563 BCE in a town that now is in Nepal near the border with India. However, India claims the faith began there because the founder's first preaching was in Benares. Hinayana Buddhism, found primarily in South Asia, stresses individual austerity and salvation by personal example. Mahayana Buddhism emphasizes salvation by faith and good works and is found in North Asia, Japan, Korea, Tibet, Mongolia, and some parts of China. Bali, Indonesia, has an interesting mix of Hinduism and Buddhism in a faith that is very much lived, not just "practiced."

The Muslim religion probably needs little introduction since it is the fastest growing faith in the USA. As you probably are aware it venerates a single, all-powerful God. Founder Mohammed was born about 570 CE in Mecca and died in 632 CE. Revelations were to have come to him directly from the angel Gabriel. There is belief in the unity of God, prayer five times a day, almsgiving, observation of the fast of Ramadan (observed the ninth month of the Islamic calendar) and a pilgrimage to Mecca at least once during one's lifetime.

The Muslim, Jewish, and Christian faiths share a common forefather in Abraham.

Living in Two (or More) Cultures

Although most people think of immigrants or expatriates when they consider the idea of having to adjust to two cultures and maintain some personal integrity, you can also be a part of two cultures for ethnic, racial, or very personal reasons.

Regarding the personal issues, sometimes called co-cultures, you may already know about some personally. Students reading this book may have contacted university student affairs departments because of a disability, maybe with learning or some physical issues that complicate their education. Educational institutions in the USA are legally required to meet student needs. However, some students may have other personal issues that they don't want to share, such as a mental illness that they may or may not let their school know about. Still others may have a same gender preference that they are open about and join organizations whose members share their situation or empathize with it, while others do not want a larger society to know in order to protect their privacy.

Students have contact with international students from other countries and probably since their first educational experiences have known students who either are immigrants or whose parents are. Still others may be members of a family whose parents have jobs abroad that has meant they have lived in and attended school in countries other than their own. Many high school and university students have educational experiences in other countries through exchange programs. These experiences all create an understanding of living in two cultures.

Expatriates who live and work in another country must either adapt or go home. Multinationals lose many of their employees on international assignments because either the employee or family members cannot adjust. Cross-cultural adaptation or acculturation seems to account for most of the successful experiences. Acculturation depends on acceptance of and adaptation to another set of values, which includes attitudes and behavior. This may depend to a great extent on the degree of difference, how receptive the host culture is, and how much exposure you have, because that increases the need for conformity and your own level of comfort with ambiguity. While a number of theorists have examined acculturation, basically it involves adaptation and your own personal degree of flexibility.

The Internet has helped with acculturation by reducing the loss of contact with your own culture, thus reducing isolation as well as offering some help with coping in the new environment. People who deal most successfully with a new culture are those with some interpersonal contacts to whom they can turn for advice and guidance to relieve the tensions of uncertainty. The Internet now has some websites to aid that process. A good example is Unknown Space LLC, an online billboard set up in 1998 for Chinese students attending American universities (Li Yuan 2004: *Wall Street Journal*, B1–2). Students can pose problems, personal or scholastic, and get advice mostly from others like them who have more experience of living in the USA.

Anyone living abroad can experience some culture shock in returning to their own culture, not only because of their readaptation but also because that culture has "moved on" while they have been gone, changing in some ways that are unfamiliar and may create anxiety and discontent.

Living in another culture long term, what most second-generation immigrants must do, usually results in assimilation. In that process, people from another culture relinquish their own culture for that of the host culture. The degree with which they are able to do this often depends upon the longevity of their parents who are most likely to cling to their own culture.

Summary

Knowledge from education or experience modifies emotional frames of reference to symbols or stereotypes. Although images give us instant recognition of an organization, product, or lifestyle, what we know objectively makes our reaction both intellectual and emotional. The persuasive nature of an image depends a great deal on our affinity for the image and what it represents to us. The more we like something, the more quickly we respond. Negative connotations can evoke hostile reactions when we see an image that represents something we don't like from exposure to information or from experience. Part of that negative response may represent a cultural conflict that has its roots in our value system.

Living in two cultures doesn't depend entirely on having another national or racial origin. You may be part of a fourth of the US population with a mental illness and have to contend with discrimination because of that. Or you may have a same gender preference and that also triggers a response. Your faith may require some dress that calls attention to your faith in a way that elicits a reaction. Most experiences, though, come from immigrants to another country who must learn to live in that culture while maintaining their own culture to preserve self-identification. Our language also creates and maintains our social reality because what we call things influences our behavior toward them (Littlejohn 2002: 164).

Further reading

See Samovar and Porter (2003) and Varner and Beamer (2001). However, the area is changing so rapidly, that you should access the Internet and carry out a search on "intercultural communication."

Discussion questions

1 If you have lived in different parts of the USA, what assumptions did you make about a place that changed after you lived there?
2 Have you ever visited another religious faith either as a guest of a friend or to attend a ceremony such as a wedding or a funeral? What seemed different to you? Did the experience change the way you thought about the faith? If so, how?
3 Have you been a guest for a special holiday or celebration in another home where you found your expectations changed because of some assumptions you had made? If so, what were the differences that you noticed and that changed your frame of reference?
4 Have you ever gone somewhere dressed in a way that seemed out of place after you arrived? What reactions did you notice in people who encountered you? Did you feel uncomfortable?

Research assignments

1 Look up the values reflected in lifestyles in different parts of the USA, or even different groups of people you are aware of. What are the sources of those values? Look up the history of the regions or the groups to see if you can find something in the background or experiences that affected values.
2 Do some research on dialects in the USA to see how these developed and whether or not they have changed over time. How do dialects affect the way others see that person?

Group discussions

1 Have you ever had someone make assumptions about you? What were they? How did you learn of the assumptions? What occurred? What changed?
2 Have you ever been assigned a roommate, either at a school or at a camp or perhaps even more briefly, such as for a retreat, and had your assumptions about that person change after the experience? Do you think their expectations of you changed? What did you learn from that?
3 If you enjoy a particular sport, does that sport have a "culture" of its own? If so, what is it? How can you recognize someone new to the sport, other than by the degree of their expertise?

Chapter 10

Ethical Issues

Eternal truths will be neither true nor eternal unless they have fresh meaning for every new social situation. (Franklin Delano Roosevelt in a September 20, 1940 address at the University of Pennsylvania, USA)

Objectives

- To consider how values shape what is considered ethical.
- To understand how perspective affects a view of what represents ethical behavior.
- To examine some basic "truths" that have universal acceptance.
- To think about the development of a worldview of ethics.

In the previous chapter (9), we considered the different values held by different cultures in a very general way. While it is important to remember that no homogeneity exists for any public, cultural norms do create generally shared sensitivities, and affect the way we interpret behaviors and events.

Values influence the way we think and thus are reflected most strongly in our beliefs, but also in our attitudes and opinions. Attitudes and opinions are words that often are used as synonyms, but aren't. Attitudes are a state of mind, a tendency or an orientation toward something or someone. An attitude is a disposition toward something or a position. You can hold an attitude that you never express. When you express a point of view, then you are giving your opinion about something or someone. Your opinions reflect your belief system because that colors your perception of information, people, and events. Beliefs are convictions that are rooted in values so that these embody one's sense of truth.

Values we hold can be personal, chosen from our culture and experience, and provide guidelines for the way we live our lives. Other values are shared with our dominant culture, and even develop in co-cultures – a minority culture within

a dominant culture. All values are learned. Cultural values originate in the philosophical issues that a culture has considered and then defined, such as what's right
and wrong, true or false, worthwhile or not. Because our values affect the way
we think and, thus, behave, these are the prisms through which we view the world.

Other influences on our values come from our age, gender, and interests. Think
of how our interests and our occupations affect our values. A bird watcher, a golfer,
a gardener have special interests that affect their sensitivities. A concert pianist, an
opera singer, a rancher, a financier, a retail manager, and an endless number of
other occupations have a work culture that they share with others in their field
wherever they live. Values, though, are not universal per se because they are learned.

However, we do have something called, for lack of a better term, a worldview.
While it really defies a clear definition, it is a way of considering the universe
and the role of humans in it. Recently many expressions of planet earth, one world,
our island in the universe and such have reflected an increasing awareness of
the fragility of our natural environment. Likewise, some efforts have been made
by news media throughout the world to think about global ethics. However,
the way different people and different individuals view the relationship of
communication and behavior has much to do with their frames of reference
(chapter 9). Ongoing tensions in the world are created by contrasting views of
nature, technology, and science. At issue is something very basic: What is
truth? Ethical conflicts have this focus.

Sensitivities

Most of us are acutely aware of how others view us because their behavior toward
us speaks loudly and clearly. Body piercings, painting, or scarring are the most
obvious attention-getters because these are permanent indicators of how we view
ourselves. When we are in an environment where our physical decorations are
accepted, we are comfortable. But, it is easy to tell when that environment changes.
An international graduate student in a US university spent a great deal of time
explaining the patterned scarring on her face that represented not only her African
tribe, but also her family's status in that tribe. Tattoos are regarded differently,
intraculturally as well as interculturally, as are other body paintings. A woman
from India was discussing the henna painting of her hands for her wedding.
Hair colorings by both men and women also get attention, especially if these
are not natural hues. A male student with a pierced tongue as well as eyebrows
described his losing argument with his grandmother when he tried to compare
his decorations with her pierced ears.

Box 10.1 Body language and interpretation

Although Pepsi as a company has a strong record for diversity in its workforce and for creating products developed for diverse cultural palates, PepsiCo's chairman and CEO, Steve Reinemund, got an email that called his attention to an interpretation that came from a cultural reading of the situation.

After an evening with some African-American employees at the company's headquarters in Purchase, New York, he addressed some remarks to them from the patio steps. Later than evening, he got an email from one of the attendees saying that for her it was the scene of a plantation owner "lecturing his slaves from on high."

Her interpretation of the event troubled him and after thanking her for candor in expressing her feelings decided he would avoid any platform-like stance in the future.

Source: Chad Terhune, "Pepsi, Vowing Diversity Isn't Just Image Polish, Seeks Inclusive Culture," *Wall Street Journal*, "In the Lead" column, April 19, 2005, p. B1.

What we wear also is a matter of consciousness, and we are made aware of a lack of conformity almost immediately, either overly or covertly. A male tourist to a mosque in Istanbul was embarrassed to be given a sarong-like wrap-around to cover his bare legs because he was wearing shorts. A female with a short skirt got the same treatment, and she said to her companion that she thought she was dressed appropriately because her arms and head were covered. Her skirt was knee-length, so she was not. The volume of tourists had exposed the mosque attendants to a great diversity in attire, so they were prepared to offer visitors appropriate remedies so they could enter. In some places less popular to tourists, though, that would not be the case. Entrance would simply be denied. In many Western nations dark clothes, especially black, are a sign of mourning, but in parts of Asia where black is worn to weddings, white is worn to funerals. Reaction to such occurrences as inappropriate dress for occasions is often politely overlooked by hosts, but the message is delivered by their expressions.

While these are not ethical violations, they are examples of sensitivities with a strong emotional base. Ethical issues represent a lack of awareness of or insensitivity to cultural norms. Two areas open to ethical missteps or misunderstandings involve money and "facts." In the USA, we are accustomed to "tipping" for services, usually meals, but in other countries gratuities are built into the price to avoid inequities among employees. We are not accustomed, though, for paying just to get things accomplished – jobs done or sales made. A friend native to a country where bribes are the norm still feels a twinge of guilt when he has

---

Box 10.2   Web woes

The Web's ability to invade traditional media with information from "outside" sources and to spread information globally put an uncomfortable spotlight on Chinese beer, consumed not just locally.

Formaldehyde, generally known for preserving bodies, is used by Chinese beer brewers to improve color and to prevent sediment from forming during storage. Although the Chinese government permits some formaldehyde in the product, consumers outside China have complained of getting headaches from Asian beer. The USA also permits a small amount of formaldehyde in beer and some other products, but some US brewers say they don't use any.

The mumblings about the chemical in Chinese beer circulated on the Internet and then an unsigned letter to Beijing's *Global Times* was printed alongside the newspaper's expose of the use of formaldehyde by breweries. The letter claimed it was used because it was the cheapest stabilizer. The expose revealed that many Chinese beers exceed the government's limit by a factor of six.

Chinese voices on the Internet proclaimed their discontent, and this was not the first wave of electronic complaints that had grabbed the government's attention. In April 2005, the topic had been counterfeit powdered milk without the needed nutrients for infants. This time, the Chinese government's General Administration of Quality Supervision, Inspection and Quarantine conducted experiments and announced that the average formaldehyde content in Chinese beers was less than 0.9 milligrams per liter, the same as the amount the World Health Organization considers safe in drinking water.

Consumer complaints to the government are new to Chinese culture, and it is the Internet that has given them voice.

Source: Geoffrey A. Fowler and Jonathan Cheng, "Beer Buzz in China over Formaldehyde Fuels Scare," *Wall Street Journal*, July 27, 2005, p. B1, 9.

to pay them. He complained recently in a phone call that his water pump went out, and with two small children, it was imperative to get it repaired immediately. Scarcely anything where he lives is considered "urgent," so it cost him a considerable amount just to get the job considered, on top of the cost of the repair. He said he felt "dirty," because he considered this unethical. He had no alternative. It is not against the law and completely within the cultural norm.

An area fraught with ethical issues is the representation of "facts." A recent report about transparency in the mass media on a global level shows a significant difference in media practices around the world. The transparency discussion began with sources of information and the consequences for the reliability of news. Most of the "news" available globally is not a reliable version of reality from anyone's perspective. What is marginally reliable is a reflection of a version of truth. To understand that "truth," you have to be able to put it in perspective based on the source. In some countries the news media are owned by the government and facts represent a political perspective only. In other countries, it is common to pay reporters and editors to publish stories. As two scholars of the transparency issue concluded: Professional journalists and their media organizations, as well as a highly diverse priesthood of journalists in the communication reformation, will be as ethical as they want to be according to what *they* perceive to be ethics and ethical conduct. Some principles are reflected in these discussions such as humanity, credibility, reliability, and consequences (see Kruckeberg and Tsetsura 2004: 92; Ward 2005; Tsetsura 2005). Furthermore, it often is not an issue of "facts" but the interpretation of those facts (Newsom et al. 2007: 165).

Interpretations

What is honest? What is fair? What is "truthful"? Interpretations are based on values.

Consider two issues that have received worldwide attention: genetic engineering of crops and baby formula.

In the USA, genetically engineered grains are not yet permitted in the food chain, but are commonly used for animals. In one instance, in the USA, genetically engineered corn was mixed with other corn and found its way into the food chain through meal used for making tacos, tortillas, and tortilla chips. A special interest group that routinely tests products sold in supermarkets discovered the problem and made it public, causing the manufacturers to withdraw their products from supermarkets and restaurants (Shlachter 2000). In many countries, no genetically modified foods are allowed. Developers of the foods have engineered them to resist disease and pests with the idea of increasing the food supply in a world where hunger is still a major problem. So, who's right?

Infant formula became an issue involving two US companies and UNICEF when the companies offered tons of free formula to HIV-infected African mothers who could give their babies AIDS by breast-feeding them. UNICEF, the UN-member agency charged with protecting the interests of children, objected and refused to approve the gifts because the industry had been involved in what was considered abusive marketing of its products in the 1970s. On that occasion, Nestlé had given free samples of its formula to new mothers to attract them to the product. By the time the samples were all used, the mothers' milk had dried up, but the formula was costly so they often diluted it, resulting in malnourished babies. Some had mixed the formula with impure water. The results were many infant deaths and a boycott of Nestlé. Although this situation was different, the interpretation of the offer was connected to the previous experience (Freedman 2000).

Interpretations are also rooted to some extent in our attitudes toward materialism. Before the globalization of markets, the division of cultures along the lines of a cultural attitude toward material goods was much more significant. However, this change, in itself, is seen by some cultures as a threat.

Box 10.3   Trust and transparency

Although "transparency" in news media has become more of an issue in the 2000s, Bulgaria saw the need for transparency demonstrated dramatically in 1986 when Chernobyl occurred. The blow-out of a reactor in northern Ukraine's power plant sent radioactive dust all over the northern hemisphere, including the USA, but the Bulgarian government told its citizens through its news media "not to worry, no pollution." The citizens were reassured – until they accessed free media.

Four years later, after the nation was freed from Communist rule and began to make its own decisions, its citizens demanded a more open government and reliability of information from its media. These efforts are ongoing, but they have made the nation an international leader in transparency on the part of government and its news media.

Source: Katie O'Keefe, *Quill* Magazine, September 2005, pp. 14–15.

Summary

Seeking a worldview on ethical issues means understanding and respecting other cultures without adopting their values. However, this requires an open mind as well as tolerance and restraint. This is not easy when cultural values reflect what in your values are considered an abuse of nature or other people.

Ethical issues are the most difficult ones to resolve by common agreement because they represent the emotionally potent conflicts of values. Consider two aspects that are reflected in events almost every day: the treatment of women and children in various cultures. Sometimes it is a religious doctrine at the heart of the contention. Sometimes it is an economic consideration. It is always a social concern. Think too of the way different cultures treat people with disabilities. These are universal because they are part of human nature, but the treatment of the physically and mentally disadvantaged is not universal.

We look at the world from a personal perspective, a professional perspective, and a global one. In the field of communication, social responsibility is based on ethical codes of behavior that have their roots in values. With today's global connectedness, organizations trying to be socially responsible have to consider cultural conflicts that challenge us with the question of what "truth" is, and makes us answer the basic question of whether or not we can live with different versions of the truth.

The way adjustments are made in most cultures is by law, but laws also are value-laden and usually the product of the dominant culture. We don't have a world court, as such, but we have managed to consider some behaviors as so egregious that they are unacceptable in any culture. These violators are tried in The Hague. Some environmental issues are being considered by coalitions of nations and settled through treaties. Negotiation is at the core of resolving some differences, though that process itself is tied to cultural norms. Some behaviors may be changed by legal mandates, so that is our next consideration.

Further reading

See Biagi and Foxworth (1997), Chatterjee (2004), El-Astal (2005), Gould (2004), Hall (1995), Merrill (1997), and Neuliep (2003).

Discussion questions

1 When you have been in other countries, what has surprised you as being accepted behaviors that would be considered unethical in your own culture?
2 Do you have friends whose view of ethical behavior is different from yours? What are these differences? How do you accommodate the differences when you are together?
3 Do you have a different view of what is ethical from that held by your parents? Grandparents? If so, what are these differences and how do you reconcile them in your family relationships?
4 Have you ever lived with someone, such as a roommate (at school or at camp) whose view of what is ethical conflicted so much with yours that you found accommodation or even understanding difficult, if not impossible? What did you do?

Research assignments

1 Which countries have the best reputations for ethical and responsible news media not only in reporting news, but also in handling advertising and public relations material? Which have the worst?
2 Which governments have the worst reputations for abuses to its citizens? To the environment? Which have the best?

Group discussions

1 What is the greatest ethical challenge you ever encountered?
2 What ethical differences can you think of that stem from religious values?
3 How do you treat ethical conflicts when you are visiting another country?

Chapter 11

Legal Issues

There is a written and an unwritten law. The one by which we regulate our constitution in our cities is the written law; that which arises from custom is the unwritten law. (Diogenes Laertius in Plato, 51 from his The Lives and Opinions of Eminent Philosophers, *translated by Charles Duke Yonge)*

Objectives

- To develop an awareness of what legal constraints exist in different countries.
- To become sensitive to the political and economic underpinnings of legal restrictions in different nations and those of different international agreements, both economic and political.
- To think about the blurring of boundaries in a global society and what the legal consequences might be.
- To understand the application of legal restraints to communication of all types.

Two offspring of the technology that has created our global community are primarily responsible for legal issues – markets and media. Markets for investments, services, and products function under regulatory controls as do the mass media. Yet, these regulations are anything but universal in either their standards or enforcement. Two influences in the way regulations are put in place and the way they are interpreted are a country's form and style of government and that government's relationship to the dominant faith and/or value system.

As discussed in chapter 3, Politics, a form of government sets forth the country's legal system, at least the structure of it. The way that system actually works, though, is part of a country's style. Style has at least three elements. A fundamental one is how open or closed the country's communication system is. The more open systems are also more flexible in their interpretations of the law and the execution of legal standards. Listening to citizens and empowering them is part of the style, although holding citizens responsible for their actions is the counterbalance to prevent chaos. The less open the communication system, the more literal the interpretation of the laws, the less flexible the regulators and the more responsibility falls on administrators who only tolerate, and not always, responses from the citizens.

Style is also affected by the dominant culture because that sets the customs and expectations of the citizenry. Cultural books refer to the North–South divide affecting countries, and suggest climate appears to be something of a factor. Northern parts of the world are stereotyped as being more energetic, less formal and less hospitable or friendly. Southern regions are stereotyped as being more easy-going, presumably because their temperatures are warmer, but also more formal in their cultural interactions yet more friendly – an expected hospitality that has rules. References to these stereotypes still appear in factual and fictional representations, although with more global mobility, it is difficult to conceive of such preservation. Those who would confront such stereotypes are often rebutted with the idea that the culture is so embedded that the "immigrants" to another clime are acculturated or they leave.

Yet another element of style is the dominant faith in a country. Obviously that is the case in nations that have a religious-based form of government. However, it also is the case where there is legal separation of church and state, but the dominant faith exerts so strong an influence that legal interpretations of laws and the creation of new laws usually are aligned with the values of the dominant faith.

Some structured cross-country laws occur within market groups, such as the European Union (EU), North American Free Trade Agreement (NAFTA), Mercosur – the replacement for the Latin American Free Trade Agreement (LAFTA), Association of Southeast Asian Nations (ASEAN), and so on. The EU is really different, though, because it has a complex infrastructure, whereas most market treaty groups have only administrators. The EU is structured so that it offers a unified entity, contrary to the other economic market-based communities. Its unity derives from: the governing body – the European Community; the Council of Ministers; a directly elected European Parliament; the European Court of Justice; and the European Conference, comprised of admitted nations. Nevertheless, the EU has not been successful in forming a unified legal system. However, its legal restrictions on biotechnical products have hit everything from crops to products.

Since we know more about the EU, it is helpful to examine the role of some of these other market communities due to their laws that do impact markets and the free trade of goods across borders. CARICOM is the Caribbean

Community and Common Market, which includes 15 nations, the largest being Jamaica. Caricom was created in 1975, and all 15 of its members have resumed normal diplomatic and market relationships with Cuba. In fact, Jamaica's prime minister visited Cuba in 1997, the first official from his country to visit the island nation in 20 years. Caricom is also a member of the 25-nation association of Caribbean states, which links it to other non-English speaking area nations. Caricom, though, has been called more of a cartel than a free trade zone because its regulations set so many fees and minimum prices.

The Central American Common Market (CACM), has existed since 1960 and includes Guatemala, Honduras, El Salvador, Nicaragua, and Costa Rica. Its protective measures for nations restrict some sales for market protection, such as the fact that Salvadoran beer is not sold in Nicaragua to protect that market. In 2005, the USA considered a trade agreement with the Central American states (CAFTA) that was opposed by some US congressional members because of non-market-driven legal agreements. The Andean Community grew out of the Andean Pact, formed in 1969 under the Cartagena Agreement, and includes Venezuela, Colombia, Peru, Bolivia, and Ecuador. This market group agreed to work with Mercosur, largely as a result of the EU's introduction of a single currency, the euro. Mercosur includes Brazil, Argentina, Paraguay, and Uruguay with Chile and Bolivia as association members. This trade group promotes the flow of goods and services past customs officials in the trade group. Furthermore, hubs for transportation systems to and from all South American nations are being developed outside of Miami, Florida, USA, which has for years provided the infrastructure needed for moving goods.

NAFTA was signed in 1994 by the USA, Canada, and Mexico, but has resulted more in a strengthening of trade with Mexico than Canada, which has more difficulty agreeing with the USA on trade rules. The free flow of goods and people across these borders has tightened since the terrorist attacks on the USA on September 11, 2001. Discussions continue for a Free Trade Area of the Americas (FTAA).

ASEAN includes Indonesia, Malaysia, the Philippines, Singapore, Brunei, Cambodia, Laos, Myanamar (formerly Burma), Thailand, and Vietnam. ASEAN ministers have been concerned about Myanmar's restrictive policies, the heroin trade and a growing AIDS problem, which has also affected member nations Vietnam, China, and India. Indonesia's instability also has been a concern, but these nations that are a part of the Asian-Pacific Economic Cooperation Group are working to eliminate laws that hamper trade and pave the way for more economic cooperation so that the market community will have more power.

Other groups that are not necessarily market communities, but do wield economic and political power include the Organization of African Unity (OAU), and the Arab League. Africa does have an Economic Community of West African States that includes Burkina Faso, The Gambia, Guinea, Ghana, Liberia, Mali, Nigeria, Senegal, and Sierra Leone. The Arab League and the OAU both have been more involved in political affairs than economic ones. For example, the Arab League has sought protections for Palestinians under Israeli governance. A name we all recognize is OPEC, the Organization of Petroleum Exporting Countries, that includes Algeria, Gabon, Indonesia, Iran, Iraq (not participating currently), Kuwait, Libya, Nigeria, Qatar, Saudi Arabia, the United Arab Emirates, and Venezuela.

The reason these economic market organizations are "legal" players is that their treaties have agreements that are legally valid and must be observed. The best evidence of this is the EU, which has Conference agreements on transportation, the environment, foreign policy, fighting crime, and such things as standards for products to be made and distributed. The product stipulations include all products to be sold in the EU nations.

Even more evidence of the legal aspects of the agreement is the EU passport acceptance. Entering EU countries, you will find one entrance marked "EU Members," where you can just walk through if you have a passport issued by an EU member nation. The other entrance is marked "Other," and that is where passports, visas, and other credentials are examined.

Government

Governments can promote or impede communication among nations. For example, since 15 of the 19 hijackers on September 11, 2001 were citizens of Saudi Arabia, that country has spent millions on public relations, advertising, and lobbying in the USA to persuade this country's citizens that all Saudis are not terrorists and that their nation doesn't support terrorism. Most of the money went into television, radio, and print ads in 20 major markets around the country. The law and lobbying firms were retained to look out for and to advance the interests of the nation in the USA's legal processes.[1]

---

[1] The promotional campaign was handled by a Virginia-based public relations firm, Qorvis Communications. One lobbying firm is headed by former US representative Thomas Loeffler, and the other lobbying was done by the law firm Patton Boggs. The monitoring of congressional and administrative policies was handled by the law firm Dutton & Dutton. From an Associated Press report accessed October 29, 2003.

Regulations can also constrain promotional efforts, as US advertisers have found out from their efforts in China. Until 2005, China's regulators were more casual about their oversight of packaging and television commercials and not as restrictive as some other countries. Now, though, the Chinese regulators are demanding proof of advertising claims, especially for consumer products. Procter & Gamble has paid a $24,000 fine to the Administration of Industry and Commerce in Nanchang province about skin cream claims and had four products banned or placed under investigation in Zhejiang province until advertising claims could be proved. The actions were taken based on a 1995 law against false and illegal claims that says all statistics and statements have to be supported by clearly indicated sources. The P&G problems centered on a shampoo, Pantene – claimed to make hair ten times stronger – and a SK-II skin cream that claims to make someone look 12 years younger in 28 days. The $100 cream also caused pain and itching. Complaints by consumers brought the products to regulators' attention, and the focus of the crackdown seems to be primarily on cosmetics. The attention seems to come from a combination of more aggressive news media and more consumer activists groups in China, according to a professor of marketing at Shanghai's China Europe International Business School (Cheng 2005).

China also has been busy trying to get a grasp of the news media. In 2005 the country's leadership limited non-national companies to one production joint venture; required the registration of broadcast equipment; banned local broadcasters from leasing channels to foreign companies; stopped giving permission to new non-Chinese satellite TV channels (arresting a plan by News Corp. to add a TV Channel with heavy Chinese-language programming) and imposed new regulations on news websites restricting them to posting only news on current events and politics, but didn't define "unacceptable subjects."

Learning to keep up with regulations in two nations as different as Japan and France will be the job of Carlos Ghosen, who will be running two auto companies at once – Nissan Motor Co. in Japan and Renault in France. Renault owns 44 percent of Nissan. Ghosen's reputation for increasing profits and operating with "flash, marketing and personal appeal," put him in this world-straddling position (Wrighton and Sapsford 2005). While this is rare for a CEO, it is not as uncommon among communicators, especially those in advertising/marketing and public relations, as many firms have offices around the world.

Among the global media, regulations for Internet content are causing a host of problems. The easy transfer of words, pictures, and sound has created a flurry of copyright lawsuits, many of which are not supportable, especially in some nations that don't recognize or respect creative property rights. In the USA, internally, there also has been some confusion about who owns what. Until

Box 11.1 Corporate free speech

A case in which Nike became involved in 1996 and 1997 when it was accused of poor working conditions and other questionable labor practices in its factories located in Thailand, Indonesia, and China came to the Superior Court of California as a result of the company's attempt to repair damage to its reputation.

Nike's campaign involved news releases, full-page ads, advertorials, and letters to the editors of major newspapers. The campaign aroused California activist Marc Kasky to file suit against Nike for unlawful and unfair business practices, saying it had misled consumers. Kasky filed the suit in California because Nike sells products there, although the company is based in Oregon. The California court didn't rule on the misleading charge, but it did rule, in a 4–3 decision, that Nike's campaign constituted commercial speech, making it subject to California's consumer protection and truth in advertising laws. The Public Relations Society of America (PRSA) filed a "friend of the court" brief saying that the ruling threatened commercial free speech.

The case moved to the US Supreme Court where the court refused to hear the case and remanded it to the California Supreme Court. That leaves a three-question test posed by Judge Joyce Kennard as precedent for testing commercial free speech. She noted that in previous rulings, the US Supreme Court had given these distinctions between commercial and noncommercial speech: (1) In commercial speech the facts are easily verifiable; (2) in commercial speech the speakers are acting from a profit position; (3) government authority is justified by regulated commercial transactions to prevent commercial harm. Therefore, she said in making a distinction what must be considered are: (1) the speaker; (2) the intended audience; (3) the content of the message. The Nike campaign, she said, was thus commercial speech, and commercial speech that is false or misleading is not protected under the First Amendment. It was her ruling that made Nike appeal to the US Supreme Court, which refused on a 6 to 3 vote to hear the case.

In 2003, Kasky and Nike, Inc. settled when Nike agreed to donate $1.5 million to the Fair Labor Association that is to use the funds for education and economic development.

Box 11.2 Product/name protection

The name for the ice cream is the same, Michoacana, and the slogan too, "es natural." The logo with a little girl in a pink dress holding an ice cream cone is a look alike as well. However, one is a US product and the other, Mexican. The Mexican originators of the brand say the brand is registered in Mexico, but not in the USA. The US company is located in Modesto, California and was begun by a Mexican immigrant. The US company's website says the brand is a family company founded in Tocumbo, Michoacán, in the 1940s, a statement that seems to confuse the issue, although the company's explanation is that the ice cream treats are produced in the Mexican style and used a name they realized Mexicans would know. The US company trademarked the name in 2003 after it experienced some imitators in the USA, and the registration was not contested by the Mexican company.

In another ice cream conflict, in 2000, the Philippine company, San Miguel, lost its legal battle to stop an Oakland, California, company from selling Magnolia, a brand name that San Miguel owns. California's Ramar company uses almost the same logo too and sells nearly identical flavors, but San Miguel had not registered its trademark abroad, so it finally dropped the case. These situations could be called unethical, but they are not illegal, and are only two examples of many "piracy" claims by companies in one part of the world that find a "twin" in another.

Source: Joel Millman, "Now, Complaints of Brand-Name 'Piracy' Go Both Ways," *Wall Street Journal*, July 11, 2005, p. B1.

---

freelance writers for newspapers and magazines complained, with lawsuits, media who had paid the freelancers for their work assumed that the purchase included use of the work on their electronic sites. Wrong. The courts decided that the freelancers were entitled to additional compensation.

Singapore scholar Ang Peng Hwa listed five areas for potential liability, especially to the server that is liable for third party content: (1) copyrighted material; (2) illegal and harmful content; (3) private and defamatory material; (4) misrepresentations; and (5) other. Under copyright, he includes one of the most prevalent and costly being the downloading of software. The illegal and harmful content includes pornography, racist, or terrorist materials. Private and

---

Box 11.3 Exporting legal work

A global marketplace has also had an impact on legal structures. One is obvious in the laws governing commerce that have been established by various economic unions. The other is virtually invisible because it is the exporting of legal work to other parts of the world.

The USA sends much of its legal work to India. Although the practice began with some basic word processing and filing that can be done by non-lawyers, it soon accelerated to research assignments that required more legal talent, and now it includes actual legal work from commercial, such as patent applications, to personal, such as divorce papers.

The legal system in India, like that of the UK and USA, is based on British common law, which means that Indian lawyers don't need much training or guidance in working for a US client law firm. Like much of the out-sourcing, legal work is cheaper in India because the charges are lower and the pool of talent is enormous. More than 200,000 Indians graduate from law school every year. While some worry about the risks, like most other outsourcing, the bottom line is driving the outsourcing.

Source: Eric Bellman and Nathan Koppel, "More U.S. Legal Work Moves to India's Low Cost Lawyers," *Wall Street Journal*, September 28, 2005, pp. B1, 2.

---

defamatory material includes such violations of privacy as posting photographs, without permission, on websites or in interactive sites such as chat rooms. Defamatory material is subject to different countries' interpretations of defamation and laws covering it. Misrepresentation is when false information is posted that damages a third party. The "other" category includes an intermediary's respons-ibility for infringements of trademarks or patents or other unfair trade practices. Of these five, Dr. Ang says, copyright and defamation can cause the most dam-age, especially copyright because it can carry a criminal penalty (Ang 2004).

Some countries, like China, block access to what the government considers "objectionable" content. Other countries such as France have gone after search engines and servers for delivering content that is not legal there. A US-based international car rental firm examined laws in 52 countries before advertising in any of them to be sure of compliance with age, insurance, licensing of drivers, and so on. Legally the global marketplace is a minefield, and not far behind it for danger is religion.

Religion

A faith affects law significantly when it is the national law, as is the case with some Islamic nations. However, it also has a strong influence on the law when it is the official religion of a country.

For example, Israel is a multiparty republic with one legislative house (the Knesset), but that doesn't mean that you can ignore the fact that most foods advertised and sold there should be marked either kosher, for the Jewish community, or halal, for the Moslem community. Both faiths do not eat pork, so products with pork content or flavors are not likely to be offered, but they are not illegal.

Malaysia is a federal constitutional monarchy with two legislative branches, a Senate and a House of Representatives, but the official religion is Islam. So, you can find some laws governing products offered, promoted, and advertised. The official name for Pakistan, though, is the Islamic Republic of Pakistan, although it has a president and a prime minister and is a military-backed constitutional regime with two legislative houses, the Senate and the National Assembly. There are many other countries where Islam is the official religion. That makes a significant difference because religious courts are the first recourse, then, perhaps, governmental courts, where these exist. Another consideration is which segment dominates: the Shiites or the Sunnis.

India is a democracy, but its official name is Bharat (Hindi). The government is a multiparty federal republic with two legislative bodies: the Council of States and the House of the People. Hindus do not eat beef, and the Moslems who live there don't eat pork. But there is no official religion. Bali, on the other hand, is in Indonesia, which is a unitary, multiparty republic with two houses – a People's Consultative Assembly and a House of the People – with a president, and proclaims its official religion as monotheism. However, in Bali, what you see practiced is an interesting mix of Hinduism and Buddhism.

Buddhism is the official religion of Thailand, though, which is a constitutional monarchy with a Senate and a House of Representatives, and a king as chief of state. You'll also find Buddhism practiced in India, where it originated; Malaysia, which has Islam as its official religion; Cambodia, where it is the official religion; the Kingdom of Bhutan where Mahayana Buddhism is the official language; and Sri Lanka, which has no official religion and is a democratic socialist republic with a president and a prime minister and is a unitary, multiparty state with one legislative house, Parliament.

What about the Catholics? The official religion of Greece is Eastern Orthodox, and Roman Catholicism is the official religion of Argentina, Bolivia, Costa Rica,

Malta, Monaco, and Peru. And the Protestants? Evangelical Lutheran is the official religion of Denmark, Faroe Islands, Greenland, Iceland, and Norway.

Confused? Of course. Where no official religion exists by mandate, it is instructive to look at the major religions represented there. Usually it is local customs that dictate such things as food, fashion, flowers, attitudes toward animals (especially dogs), representations of people and use of hands and feet, but not always.

Summary

It is instructive to look at how we arrived at this global tangle of laws and values. In the early 1970s conventional television signals began taking advantage of satellites. Intelsat (International Telecommunications Satellite Consortium) was formed for all non-Soviet, non-military international satellite communications and a private US government regulated corporation, Comsat (Communication Satellite Corporation) was formed to manage and operate the satellites. Two men who took advantage of this new opportunity for television were Rupert Murdoch and Ted Turner. Australian Murdoch was already a significant publisher in his own country and in the United Kingdom before he bought STAR-TV and Fox network. Ted Turner founded Turner Broadcasting System and introduced CNN. In response to outcries about the negative effect these intruders would have on local broadcasting, many governments anted up and supplied more government money so the local networks could compete and provided additional resources to improve local programming.

Also in the 1970s, building on the 1960s connection of computers by the scientific community to expedite communication, electronic messaging (email) began. By the 1980s researchers, academicians, and government officials were routinely exchanging information via computer. The 1990s opened up the Internet to use by a larger public by the advent of the World Wide Web that allowed for the transfer of graphics, video, and sound. By 1997, advertising on the Web moved beyond the display of names and products to incorporate dialogue and motion and the investment reached $400 million. Intermercials were introduced. These four-minute communications drew their name from interstitials, a form of Web advertising in which the advertiser's message automatically pops up in front of a user while the browser is downloading a page within a site. In 2005, Yahoo developed a plan to put a digital library of copyrighted books, video/audios, and academic papers online, after gaining permission from authors and publishers. Although Yahoo will have its own search engine (www.opencontentalliance.org), the material will be accessible by other search engines such as Google's. Google ran into copyright restrictions in its effort to build an online library but probably will continue those efforts too. The impetus for digital access is there. Although some online content is copyrighted, much is not. The Google situation has resulted in legal action by major publishers, and a final decision on that case may set the boundaries for all copyright issues on the Internet (Delaney and Trachtenberg 2005).

The newest mass medium is also the freest, because most of its content has no editors. It also allows for international discourse in "real time." For companies it offers both intranet and extranet opportunities, and supplies a place for business transactions of all kinds on a global level. The opportunities continue to expand, and as they do they outweigh the hazards.

Further reading

See Reus-Smit (2004). For additional information, given the political and religious upheavals, even in the USA, I suggest depending on the Internet for updates.

Discussion questions

1   What freedoms do you think people should have wherever they live?
2   What countries restrict some of those freedoms? Why might that be?
3   What specific types of communication can laws restrict?

Research assignments

1   Look up various efforts to develop international laws and their enforcement, historically. What were the efforts and the results?
2   How do religious-based legal systems differ from secular ones?

Group discussions

1   Have you ever been in a country where you felt uncomfortable or even fearful of violating a law?
2   What examples of "unwritten" laws can you think of, and what are the consequences of violating these?
3   What might be the future of some international legal system? How might it be enforced?

Chapter 12

The Roles of Advertising and Public Relations

Public opinion's always in advance of the law. (John Galsworthy in Windows, Act 1)

Objectives

- To become sensitive to differences in the way communication practitioners are educated for and handle their practice in different parts of the world.
- To develop tactics to accomplish communication tasks successfully across borders.
- To understand how different techniques can be used to accomplish goals and to be able to bring creativity to address opportunities and problems.

Although a global marketplace creates more opportunities and necessities for advertising and public relations practitioners around the world to work together, opportunities for mistakes and misunderstandings to arise also are increased. In launching campaigns, either commercial or nonprofit, the common practice is for a universal theme to be developed and then adaptations made for the different sites. Generally that means coordinating and cooperating countless details across political and cultural borders. In some cases, a diversity in the home office has helped identify partners abroad because many families that have immigrated remain in contact with relatives and friends in their country of origin. Their children "inherit" their extended family as well as their distant relatives. Some of the most successful partnering has resulted from such interpersonal relationships. However, often that opportunity does not exist and some "partnering" is a business arrangement that needs closer examinations for success.

The first step for the practitioners is getting to know their counterparts. Roles are not the same around the world. Although advertising jobs are more likely to be parallel than public relations ones, still media are structured differently and function in a cultural climate that places some boundaries on what can be said and displayed.

Among the first questions to ask is the background of your counterpart. In the USA, some college preparation is involved for advertising and public relations jobs. Although that is increasingly the case in other countries, many or even most were trained in the workplace. The differences usually involve an approach to strategies and to measurement. Theoretical bases for strategy may be unfamiliar as are scientific measurements for baselines, progress, and final evaluation of behavior change.

Another question to ask is the counterparts' job description and the accountability or reporting hierarchy. That will determine how many decisions have to be approved at different levels. Any campaign has four major components: creative talent, technical skills, time deadlines, and costs. Understandings will have to be reached on each.

An interesting aspect of creativity involved a thinking process that seems to have no geographical origin. In the USA, it has been called "thinking outside the box." The origin of this may be in the work of Edward de Bono, who wrote *Lateral Thinking for Management: A Handbook for Creativity* in 1971 that was published by the American Management Association. De Bono has turned this into a major industry that is easy to find by Googling his name. His concept is that thinking laterally involves the right side of the brain, the emotional side. This is different from vertical or left brain thinking that tends to be logical and analytical. Picking up on this, Philip Carter and Ken Russell developed psychometric testing to measure personality, intelligence, creativity, and lateral thinking. (See their 2003 book, *More Psychometric Testing: 1000 New Ways to Assess Your Personality, Creativity, Intelligence and Lateral Thinking.*)

The lateral thinking concept was taken a step further by John O'Keeffe, who wrote *Business Beyond the Box* in 1998 where he suggests that only triangular thinking helps realize goals. He sees the vertical thinking where people with information move to think laterally, creatively, unite these two with a baseline of a goal to form a triangle and employ the whole brain. Another aspect of this is that because in lateral thinking, the right side – emotional side – of the brain is involved, the thought process is not as predictable as when both sides of the brain work together.

Creative talent is needed locally to interpret the campaign and adapt it to local customs for clothing, colors, symbols, language, and gestures. Technical talent necessary to produce the materials may be available "in-house" or may have to be contracted out to others. Understandings about time affect deadlines, and have to consider cultural differences. Each of these involves money. Who has the ability to approve expenses has to be clear – not always easy when the power to make commitments isn't apparent. Discovering answers to all of these questions, while not simple, is the framework on which work for the campaign must be built.

Advertising

Appeals have two components: illustrations and product information. Unquestionably the most sensitive of these are the illustrations. Product information is largely controlled by law – what you must say, what you may not say. However, you get little help with how literally what you say may be interpreted and how much puffery pushes the ad into a legal action.

Advertising campaigns are the most likely to be able to "go global" with few changes. Appeals are usually emotional and depend upon some recognition of the product, or the product category. Think of cell phones (mobiles), computers, CDs, cameras, cars and their components such as tires, crops such as rice, coffee and tea, tools, jewelry, flowers, bread, most produce. If the illustration is culturally acceptable, you'll be okay.

Illustrations

Most Moslem countries are sensitive about any artistic representation of the human body. How that body is clothed is another consideration. Nudity or even generous exposure will create problems in a number of countries, while in others exposure even of genitalia doesn't cause concern.

Figure 12.1   Cottonelle (Kimberley-Clark) ad in French

Costumes for advertising models are always an issue. The way a sari is wrapped carries many messages and a kimono wrapped right over left is only for a corpse. For male models it is easier because Western-styled clothes are worn in many parts of the world. Head coverings for both genders need to be culturally correct, and also the posture for hands and feet. Views of the soles of the feet are usually not acceptable, and the left hand is seen as unclean in many cultures. It is not uncommon for a single commercial in India to involve four or five costume changes and be prepared in 16 different languages.

In India, as well as some other countries, liquor cannot be show in an ad, so what you may see is an ad with different containers represented and some vague copy that is meaningful only if you know what the unnamed product is.

Product information

Your ad may be selling a specific product or an idea. Products are easier because laws control much of the content. In the USA, product ingredients are required

Figure 12.2 Coca-Cola Billboard

and drugs must have dense copy, usually in small type, that describes the hazards and side effects of taking the medication. Copy for cigarette advertising, in the limited places it is permitted, also must carry warnings.

Technical products are easier to write about because consumers want to know those details and are usually knowledgeable enough to understand direct translations. It is the emotional copy that is likely to cause trouble, primarily because allusions are used. Hair products and perfumes are a challenge because of cultural preferences and understandings. Humor is risky and innuendos even more so. The copy for some British ads employing a double entendre would not pass the "taste test" in the USA.

Products seem to stand on their own merits, with good advertising support, maintaining a loyal audience even when customers are unhappy with the political policies of the country associated with their origin. The identification

---

Box 12.1 Brand and country of origin connections

Although surveys of consumers in France and Germany by Edelman Public Relations indicated that consumers said they were less likely to buy American products due to opposition to the US-led war in Iraq, what consumers say and what they do seem to be different. Frustration with foreign policy hasn't come between consumers and some of their favorite brands. According to a survey about the same time, 2004, by Research International of London, the "least cool celebrity" is US President George Bush, but the "coolest" fashion brand is Levi's. Levi, though, abandoned its US imagery and identification in Europe long before the Iraq war.

However, in some countries what seems to make a difference is a local source for a product. In Turkey where sensitivity to US foreign policy is likely to be higher, a Turkish food company, the Ulker Group, began selling Cola Turka, a competing product for Coca-Cola and Pepsi, and with a strong advertising campaign by the WPP Group captured 20 percent of Turkish cola sales in six months.

Source: Guy de Jonquières, "Dislike of Regimes Colours Consumer Attitudes", *Financial Times*, London, January 12, 2004; Eric Pfanner, "Anti-U.S. Ads Break Taboo over Politics," *International Herald Tribune*, January 19, 2004 and Eric Pfanner, "Concern About U.S. Foreign Policy Has Some Re-Evaluating Ad Tactics," *New York Times*, London edition, January 20, 2004.

with their country of origin almost always becomes a political issue, though. Americans annoyed with the French for not supporting the invasion of Iraq wanted to rename "French fries," or just call them "fries," and over the years some McDonald's restaurants suffered mob damage in several countries where America's foreign policy was in disfavor. However, when the product is advertised with a local touch, and sometimes when it isn't, a good product seems resilient (see Box 12.1).

Public Relations

As a function of management, public relations is charged with helping an organization, one the PR practitioner works for internally or externally in servicing a client, to represent its mission by what it says and does. In doing so, PR is charged with developing long- and short-term strategies and tactics that advance the organization while projecting and protecting its reputation and credibility. A PR person has to be part of the management team as a counselor in order to advise and guide policies that are in the best interests of the publics the organization serves. This is not always easy since publics often have conflicting goals. In a global society what is most critical is that an organization's public relations practitioners have a seamless and fluid world culture. The real key here is a continuous flow of information so no one in the organization is surprised and everyone is constantly updated across time zones, languages, customs and local social, economic and political environments (Mitchell 2004: 18). This is easier said than done, and while technology helps, nothing substitutes for some experience at other sites so you get to know your colleagues and gain some sense of the climate in which they are working. Another help are national and international public relations organizations. Membership in these for the public relations staff in other countries helps unify concepts of public relations practice and assure some level of professionalism.

Policies

Consistency with organizational practices and a thorough understanding of the corporate culture is essential to preserve the integrity of the organization. Anytime that an organization has a problem anywhere in the world, it reflects on the whole organization and all of its offices. For that reason, the PR practitioners around the world must be excellent issues identifiers and managers so they can anticipate problems and alert the home office to situations that might cause a triggering

---

Box 12.2 Rules for success in the global marketplace

Five rules that most multinationals have found that seems to work best in a global marketplace are:

1 Integrate public relations and advertising perhaps in a separate multi-cultural department because the editorial and advertising lines are often blurred, especially in ethnic media.
2 Do your research of media outlets so you understand language, content, deadlines and contacts (even in the USA where there are more than 700 Spanish-language newspapers and more than 600 Asian-language media).
3 Connect with the culture so that you understand the values, community, lifestyles, religion, ethnicity, race, sexual orientation, class, country of origin and degree of acculturation, which affects every aspect of the media mix.
4 Remember that perception is always reality, in this case the way the community sees a company influences how individuals view it.
5 Partner with experts who know the market and locate a guide through *The Source Book of Multicultural Experts*, published by Multicultural Marketing Resources, Inc.

Source: Gina Rudan (director of multicultural and international markets for PR Newswire), in PRSA's *Tactics*, August 2004, p. 19. © 2004 *PR Tactics*. Reprinted with permission by the Public Relations Society of America, www.prsa.org.

---

event that precipitates a crisis. Planning beats coping every time. Perception of potential problems helps control the response so that credibility and reputation are maintained. A crucial role for the on-site PR people is to keep the home office PR person, and thus the whole management team, aware so that no-one gets surprised. Keeping the home office aware of and sensitive to potential cultural clashes is one of the most important roles for the on-site PR people.

Practices

While policies such as employee compensation, gender roles, minority publics, and child labor are almost always culture landmines, some practices may be too. One of the most common areas for conflict is transparency, as mentioned in

Chapter 10. Bribes are a way of doing business in many places around the world, but US citizens engaging in such activities anywhere can be sent to a federal prison, something scarcely worth the risk, local practice or not. A more subtle sort of situation occurs with a practice that the Chinese call "guanxi." The word has no English equivalent. The Chinese try to explain it to Westerners by saying it is a personal relationship with someone in power who can help make something happen through use of power, status, and access. Reciprocity not only is expected, it is anticipated to be a return greater than the deed (Newsom et al. 2007: 14).

Other practices such as public expressions of opinion in a letter to the editor of a newspaper or writing an opinion piece for publication, or putting out a blog, while common in many countries, is likely to create an international incident in nations that have restraints on freedom of expression. EU countries, for example, don't tolerate "hate speech," and many seemingly open countries forbid any- thing even remotely critical of the national government – Singapore for example. While these are legal issues too, as covered in the previous chapter, some practices are so common in public relations that constant reminders are necessary. Public health campaigns, always launched with the best of intention, can run afoul of culturally "acceptable" communication, especially when the target is adolescents. Finding a spokesperson is not always simple either, especially when social sta- tus is a fundamental part of the culture. Often gender is an issue, but sometimes not. In Brazil, where public relations practitioners are licensed and education for the job is required, although men usually performed the higher corporate roles of ethics and social responsibility, governmental harmony, and community well- being, while women are generally in the employee well-being role, female practitioners in higher positions in the organizations performed the usually assigned male roles with the same regularity as men (Molleda and Ferguson 2004). Their higher position in the organization gave them the greater status needed to assume the usually male roles. In some countries, research on publics is growing dram- atically. In Europe, for example, there is a heavy investment in finding out about consumers because this is affecting more than just analyzing what they buy. Much of the research is psychographically driven, especially in studies of lifestyles. Such studies now are even affecting the way shopping centers are designed.

Practices, since these are tactical, usually fall into one of two subsets of pub- lic relations: media relations or publicity/promotion.

Media relations   The role of public relations in society often determines how PR efforts are accepted by the news media. Where the government owns the news media, promotional materials from government sources are taken for granted and published, but in less restricted media, the government may not get as gen- erous a treatment. For example, Korean media even have different names for the two public relations sources: "Hong Bo" for government sources and PR for corporate publicity. In the case of the Koreans, newspaper sources favor the corporate over the government (Park 2001). Yet another aspect of acceptance of public relations sources is the professionalism of local reporters and editors, although political systems appear to be more of a factor (Weaver 2004: 150).

Publicity/promotions   Many Asian nations have used publicity and promotion in campaigns for nation-building, sometimes called Development Public Relations. Campaigns directed toward its citizens are common both in Singapore where government own the news media and also in India, which has a free press. The difference is that in India, as in the USA, there may be some critical voices heard. Highly organized local activist adversaries are less likely to oppose government campaigns in Asian nations than in Western ones. That is even the case in some of the emerging democracies where a very active, and relatively free, media are growing up along with their governments.

Part of the consideration of campaigns from any source is the view of public relations as a function of democracy by stimulating public discourse on an issue. The Internet as a medium has the spotlight now because of its phenomenal growth.

Box 12.3 Literacy, a human right

A campaign to watch is the United Nations' "Literacy Decade," 2003–2012. This is a global effort through UNESCO to teach the uneducated all over the world to read so they can gain access to information. Another aspect is the hope that literacy will give these uneducated citizens of the global community the ability to express themselves and present their points of view. The notion that education increases power also is part of the effort to make the views of these people heard.

Priority will be given to females, ethnic and linguistic minorities, indigenous populations, migrants and refugees, the disabled, and children and youths. The campaign is structured around gender, poverty, health, peace, and freedom, and its implementation is set for two five-year periods.

In explaining why the campaign is scheduled for a decade, the UN cited three reasons: literacy is a human right now denied to more than 860 million adults and 113 million children not in school; literacy should at least be a choice; literacy efforts up to now have been inadequate. For background on the campaign and for updates, see the website www.unesco.com.

Anxious governments have tried to restrict citizens' access, but PR uses the Internet for product/service and other announcements as well as for making information and materials instantly available globally on websites, thereby enhancing media relations. One difficulty with the Internet is the blurring of differences between mediated communication and immediate communication, especially with the explosion of blogs. That only complicates the existing problem of information being interpreted by receivers in their cultural context, regardless of the intent.

Summary

Campaigns may be mostly advertising with some public relations tactical support. Others may be largely a public relations effort, with some promotional displays, signs, and perhaps a few ads. The success of any campaign, though, depends upon what have been called the "five Es": education, engineering, enforcement, entitlement, evaluation.

Education is just what you might expect: information that gives people knowledge they didn't have, or offers them a different perspective on an issue or a situation. If you are trying to rid areas of mosquitoes without using pesticides, then you need to tell people what they can do to help, such as getting stagnant water off their own property. *Engineering* means making it possible, even easy, for people to comply with what is being asked. For example, if you want people to have their children inoculated against childhood diseases, then you need easily accessible clinics that either are free or inexpensive. *Enforcement* can be legal or social. A good example is keeping trash out of public places. While legal authorities may impose fines, often social pressure can be brought to bear so that the desirable behavior becomes the only socially acceptable act. *Entitlement* means that the people being asked to change their behavior feel that there is value in the appeals of the campaign, and that the organization has the legitimacy to ask for their help and compliance. Entitlement is also a good example of reinforcement because people telling others extends the message. Those who have accepted the message need reminding and need reinforcement for what they are doing so they will continue that behavior. *Evaluation* is the way a campaign takes stock of its success not only while the campaign is going on, but also after it is over. The best evaluation takes a look at whose behavior changed and when, and whether or not that change is being retained and by what groups.

Internationally, the evaluation part of a campaign is the most sensitive, although the most necessary. First you need research to find out what the level of awareness of the problem is and what people think about the issue. Initial research makes it possible to set a benchmark, a clear and demonstrable baseline. You have to know where you are before you know how far you've gone toward a goal. You can't measure change without knowing where you started. Some countries are very sensitive to having members of the public questioned, and furthermore in some countries you can't even ask some members of the public, such as women or children, either or both of them, who may be the primary publics for a campaign, especially about health issues. Beyond that, many countries lack the infrastructure to give you reliable secondary research, even just statistical. Or, if the government is somewhat insecure, the information may be there but withheld for reasons of national pride or even just politics.

You must have objectives for the campaign that are realistic and achievable. Ongoing campaigns, such as health issues, will have both strategic objectives that involve behavior change and tactical objectives that measure the relative success of various persuasive efforts. An example might be looking at whether the Internet seems to be a better way to reach a large public than traditional media.

To use resources prudently, a campaign needs ongoing measurement of every stage to see what the change is from the baseline. If money is being spent on something that doesn't seem to be working, then you need to divert those resources – time, money, or people or all of these – to something more productive.

Finally, you must evaluate the entire process on three levels. First, *input* answers questions such as: Is adequate information gathered? Are channels of communication correctly chosen? Are messages presented properly? Second, *output* looks at such questions as: How many messages were sent? How many people received them? Where were the messages placed? Who considered them? Third, *outcome* examines the following: How many attitudes changed or how many responded positively to the message? How many behaved in the desired manner? What objectives were achieved?

The technical means to discover the answers to these questions exists almost everywhere now, but the constraints are cultural and political. You need to find out from your counterparts working at each site how to accomplish this. Without the information, there is no way to be accountable for the investment in the campaign or to even estimate its effectiveness.

Further reading

See Culbertson and Chen (1996), Duncan (2002), Sriramesh and Verčič (2003), Tilson and Alozie (2004), and Turk and Scanlan (2004).

Discussion questions

1 How would you go about finding a "partner" in another country where you need to launch a communication campaign?
2 What would you need to find out about that partner and how would you go about this without appearing to be intrusive?
3 What are the differences in handling a nonprofit organization's global campaign versus a commercial one?

Research assignments

1 Choose another country where you would want to launch a communication campaign and determine what you need to know before planning the campaign.
2 Choose a product that has a global market and find out how it is handled and by whom in its different markets.

Group discussions

1 What have you discovered is different about shopping centers/malls in other countries you have visited?
2 What experiences have you had with communication students from other countries? What do they see as different about advertising and public relations in the USA?
3 What nonprofit organizations have you worked with as a volunteer that also operate abroad? What are their rules, regulations, practices covering working in another country?

Chapter 13

Miscommunication and Consequences

Mishaps are like knives, that either serve us or cut us, as we grasp them by their blade or by the handle. (James Russell Lowell, in Cambridge Thirty Years Ago)

Objectives

- To watch for cultural glitches in advertising, promotions, special events, speeches, and other events to learn from others' mistakes.
- To examine ways that mistakes have been corrected and apologies made.
- To sharpen sensitivity and empathy by observing reactions to other cultural groups.
- To explore ways to avoid cultural miscues in communication.

Communication missteps can occur from nonverbal interactions – including gestures, symbols, logos, color choices – and other cultural mores, as we know from discussions in previous chapters. A powerful impact occurs when these missteps are presented in editorial content, especially in news media, or in commercial and promotional content.

News content has inflamed anger and resentment to the point that lives were lost. Commercial content has severely damaged relationships within cultures where a profit-making organization was trying to do business or a nonprofit organization was trying to function for the benefit of publics it is dedicated to serving. Such problems, once they occur, tend to resurface, either on the Internet or in later negotiations of the organization with government or indigenous commercial institutions. Nimbus publics frequently get involved and keep a controversy alive. These publics may be expatriates of the involved country, or their descendants. If a race or religion is affronted, their members around the globe share the anger or distress and keep the issue alive longer than it might be with those directly affected.

Affronts get wider distribution in this wired world through emails and Internet blogs and websites, especially those with chat rooms or other interactive components.

Mass Communication/Editorial Content

Microsoft's UK office in 2004 issued a news release about the launch of the iLoo, an Internet-enabled toilet that was supposed to allow "instant logging on."[1] The release became a joke in the US and UK media. Instead of apologizing, the company compounded the problem by claiming the release was an April Fool-like joke. However, it had to admit that the product was a real one that was killed by the company. Evite, a party-planning website, called Yom Kippur a "reason to party" in an e-newsletter, then had to apologize because the Jewish observance is a day of atonement, not a cause for celebration. The website looked especially ignorant because, as a party-planner, it is expected to understand holidays.[2]

Convenience over-ruled accuracy and the Bermuda Department of Tourism launched a new marketing campaign with a picture of a beach in Hawaii, not Bermuda. Instead of being embarrassed and apologizing, the tourism minister claimed that the stock photo was used intentionally to allow for "maximum creative impact with superior fiscal responsibility."[3] Save money, perhaps it did, but did little to "save face" or reputation.

While these are amusing, a few sentences in one edition of the US news magazine *Newsweek* created riots in the Islamic world, some resulting in deaths and injuries. The riots drew global television coverage, and the story became an international incident.

What occurred is that an article in its May 9, 2005 issue said that information from "sources" had reported that interrogators at the Guantánamo Bay, Cuba, detention center had flushed copies of the Qu'ran down the toilet to upset detainees into confessing. The story was translated into Arabic for the magazine's Arabic edition, published in partnership with Kuwait's Al-Watan Publishing Group.

Moslems all over the world were incensed by this desecration of their sacred text. The US president went on television to say no desecration of any religious text ever would be knowingly permitted or condoned by this country. Riots and protests that killed 16 occurred in Indonesia, Gaza, and Afghanistan where the

---

[1] "Did They Really Say That?" Regan's Media Relations Report, April 2004, p. 3.
[2] Ibid.
[3] Ibid.

most serious single incident occurred when the police fired on hundreds of Khogiani tribesmen who were trying to protest in Jalalabad, killing four and injuring 60. Later the president of Pakistan's Islamist Alliance called for massive rallies in five or more Muslim countries as part of an International Protest Day against the desecration of the Qu'ran.

Two weeks after the initial publication, *Newsweek* said that their report might have contained some errors because its anonymous source for the information recently told them that he didn't have first-hand knowledge of the incident, and that it may have been just a story told by former detainees. The magazine also said that a copy of the news item also had been sent to the Pentagon prior to publication, and the official to whom it was sent didn't raise any questions about the story.

The magazine didn't apologize for the story, only said it may have gotten some facts wrong, but did apologize for the violence that the story provoked in the Middle East and expressed sympathy for the victims of that violence. That letter from the editor, Mark Whitaker, was not published in the Arabic edition, but it did run a follow-up story about the fallout from the story in which it said, "radical Islamic foes . . . quickly exploited local discontent . . . and riots began breaking out last week." Subsequent *Newsweek* editions, translated from the US edition, did have an editor's note admitting fault and pledging to earn "renewed confidence" by producing the best magazine it could each week. The Arabic version did not have a copy from the US edition titled "The Qu'ran Question," which suggests the story still might be true, and the story itself was not new.

The issue didn't die, but was kept alive by continuing inquiries about the use of an anonymous source (known to the editor), the Pentagon "official" who wasn't named, and the diligence or lack thereof in attempts to verify the facts.[4]

Agenda setting is evident in the pick-up of stories that arouse public interest by media, and usually around the world. Even the Terry Schiavo case that aroused a national debate in the USA over whether the brain-dead woman should be kept alive artificially and who should make that decision, her spouse or her parents, got international coverage primarily because of the Catholic angle called into focus by her parents and Catholic priests. Likewise, stories of denial of women's rights anywhere gain international attention.

---

[4] Compiled from the following news stories: Wahid Al-Saqaf, "Newsweek Has Arabic Edition Challenge," *Wall Street Journal*, May 25, 2005, p. B2B; Carlotta Gall, "Afghanistan, Anti-American Violence Spreads to 10 Provinces," *Fort Worth Star-Telegram*, May 13, 2005, p. 25A; Joe Hagan, "Newsweek Flap Spurs Debate Over Sources," *Wall Street Journal*, May 17, 2005, p. B1, 2; Joe Hagan and Sara Schaefer-Muñoz, "Newsweek Says Article on Quran Might Have Contained Errors," *Wall Street Journal*, May 16, 2005, p. B2.

When a country is portrayed in a negative light by the coverage, the nations often complain that their country is ignored until something bad happens, and then the negative news has a permanent effect on public opinion. Some research indicates that they are correct in that negative news coverage does make it more likely that there will be a negative public perception of the country while positive coverage seems to have no effect (Wanta et al. 2004).

Commercial/Promotional Content

Ads and commercials often get more attention than other promotional content due to exposure. That was the case with a Toyota ad showing one of its four-wheel drive vehicles towing a Dongfeng (Chinese) truck. Toyota had to apologize to Chinese consumers who complained in chat rooms about the implication of a Japanese vehicle towing a Chinese one. However, one ad that never appeared in commercial media turned the tables. A Chinese trade publication, *International Advertising*, in publishing a report on the creative efforts of multinational ad agency Leo Burnett, showed a Nippon paint ad that had a dragon losing its grip and sliding down a pillar of a Chinese pavilion that was painted with Nippon paint. This flurry of complaint also appeared in the Internet, and it centered on the fact that the dragon is a symbol of Chinese culture. A Chinese creative team was responsible for the ad, but that didn't matter, and Leo Burnett China apologized to the Chinese public for the ad.[5]

Sometimes ads designed for posters and billboards don't even get the intended exposure because of ignorance about the country. It may be weather conditions or it may be something not as easily researched. For example, in India posters are often pasted on walls by unskilled workers, hired for a job. These "hoardings," as they are called, do get put up, but it may be that a few wandering goats are right behind eating the posters, because of the glue, so that the posters have a very short life.[6]

The problem in a campaign may be with translations. The Dairy Associations' well-known campaign "Got Milk?" when exported to Mexico had the unfortunate translation: "Are You Lactating?" (Ricks 2000: 86). Even when you hire a native in the language, mistranslations can occur if the translator doesn't understand the content. For example, when a freelance Arabic translator working on the

---

[5] Danwei: Media and Advertising in China, from Advertising and Media file; accessed September 28, 2004; available from http://www.danwei.org/archives/000971.html

[6] From personal experience.

Box 13.1 Adding fuel to the fire

An ad for the V-22 Osprey aircraft that flies vertically like a helicopter and horizontally like a traditional fixed wing plane created a furor with the Council on American-Islamic Relations.

The headline on the ad read: "It descends from the heavens. Ironically it unleashes hell."

The aircraft made by Boeing Co. and Bell Helicopter was advertised in the public affairs *National Journal* on September 24, and the visual showed US special operations troops rappelling out of the aircraft for an assault on a mosque.

The copy reads: "Before you hear it, you see it. By the time you see it it's too late. The CV-22 delivers Special Forces to insertion points never thought possible. It flies faster. It flies farther. It flies quieter. Consider it a gift from above."

The ad, designed by TM advertising in Irving, Texas, was supposed to have been pulled in all publications after it ran once in August. The company said previous to that publication, the ad's content had not been approved by all of the people who should have seen it.

After publication, according to Bell Helicopter's spokesman Mike Cox, directions were given to pull the ad in all other publications, but the *National Journal*, he said, did not follow those instructions.

Apologies were offered and accepted by the council, although the government affairs director for the council, Corey Saylor, said the group still questioned the motives of Bell and Boeing.

Source: Bob Cox, "Bell, Boeing Apologize for V-22 ad," *Fort Worth Star-Telegram*, October 1, 2005, pp. 1, 8C. Reprint courtesy of the *Fort Worth Star-Telegram*.

---

translation of a US computer company's manual and encountered the terms "dummy" and "load," he did find the Arabic equivalents in his dictionary, but the combination produced the Arabic term for "false pregnancy" (Ricks 2000: 86).

Sometimes the difficulty is even more basic, a translation or meaning of the name of a company or a product. Colonel Sanders' Kentucky Fried Chicken created a problem in Germany because of the association of "Colonel" with the US military, and in Brazil the pronunciation of Kentucky Fried Chicken was a problem, so just Sanders was used. An airline's firm name was EMU, but that created a problem in Australia where the emu is a bird that can't fly (Ricks 2000: 45–6).

Box 13.2 How 8 pixels cost Microsoft millions

New Delhi: Just when the antitrust case went in sleeping mode, Microsoft managed to get into yet another fiasco. This time the software giant is hit by information misrepresentation or shall we say goof up.

The lack of multicultural savvy attitude cost the software giant millions of dollars.

Microsoft products have been banned in some of the biggest markets, including India because of eight wrongly colored pixels, a bad choice of music and a bad English-to-Spanish dictionary.

Tom Edward, head of Microsoft's geopolitical strategy team told a conference in Glasgow, how one of the biggest companies in the world managed to offend one of the biggest countries in the world with a software slip-up, CNet Asia reported.

When coloring in 800,000 pixels on a map of India, Microsoft colored eight of them a different shade of green to represent the disputed Kashmiri territory. The difference in greens meant Kashmir was shown as non-Indian, and the product was promptly banned in India. Microsoft was left to recall all 200,000 copies of the offending Windows 95 operating system software to try and heal the diplomatic wounds. "It cost millions," Edwards said.

If this was not enough, Microsoft used chanting of the Koran as a soundtrack for a computer game, which led to great offence to the Saudi Arabia government. This company later issued a new version of the game without the chanting, while keeping the previous editions in circulation because US staff thought the slip wouldn't be spotted, but the Saudi government banned the game and demanded an apology. The game was then withdrawn.

The software giant managed to further offend the Saudis by creating another game in which Muslim warriors turned churches into mosques. That game was also withdrawn.

Microsoft has also managed to upset women and entire countries. A Spanish-language version of Windows XP, destined for Latin American markets, asked users to select their gender between "not specified," "male," or "bitch," because of an unfortunate error in translation.

Microsoft has also seen its unfortunate style of diplomacy have an effect in Korea, Kurdistan, Uruguay and to China – where a cartographical dispute saw Chinese employees hauled in front of the government.

Edwards said that staff members are not sent on geography courses to try to avoid such mishaps. "Some of our employees, however bright they may be, have only a hazy idea about the rest of the world," he said.

Source: Reprinted with permission from economictimes.com (accessed August 23, 2004).

Summary

As amusing as some of these examples are, it isn't a joke having to invest in corrections or launch explanations and apologies. The best approach is first to do adequate research, pretest, and ask for help from expatriates from those countries or colleagues on site.

Research is key. Selecting a global name proved successful for Kodak. A research team searched for a name that was pronounceable everywhere but had no specific meaning anywhere (Ricks 2000: 46). Multinationals, like Kodak, need to be sure that beyond the acceptability of the name the reputation of the organization needs to be maintained even with the shifting sands of the global economic, political, and social scene. This is especially important when a crisis occurs and their commitment to the community and the community's respect for the organization is challenged (Bardhan and Patwardhan 2004; Ho and Hallahan 2004).

Diversity in the USA is making such cultural explorations useful. For example, an experiment in trying to stress the importance of getting mammograms to African American women through a brochure, the researchers found that almost everything mattered: editorial approach in content, use of photos and clip art, paper texture, graphics for presentation of statistics, color and design. The culturally tailored brochure increased learning, a shift in attitude toward screening and reduction of barriers to getting mammograms (Springston and Champion 2004).

The need to culturally fine-tune communication in the US will increase with more immigrants arriving as a result of government actions. One is the 2004 decision to increase the number of visas granted for high-tech workers in such fields as architecture, engineering, medicine, biotechnology and computer programming. Another is the decision to exempt from the limit on foreign workers the foreign students with graduate degrees from US universities. The fact that cultural pockets exist in the USA is not new to a nation of immigrants, but it is telling that a website exists to help Chinese adjust and adapt to life in the USA.[7]

Management issues can also cause problems. Strategies for entering a new market were dramatically illustrated by Disney's opening a theme park in Paris. Cultural ignorance is not the only issue, though. Among the others are failure to modify products for the market, although McDonald's has success stories that you can see when you go into their restaurants in other countries and look at the menus. Personnel issues can occur with what the USA calls "downsizing,"

---

[7] http://www.mitbbs.com

the UK "redundancies," and in other cultures it is more like treason because while loyalty to the firm is expected, it is also expected to be reciprocated. Trust is critical to reputation. TrustCitigroup faced a crisis in Japan when the National Association of Securities Dealers (NASD) fined Citigroup Global Markets, Inc. for "inappropriate sales literature" that didn't include adequate risk disclosures, advertised a target rate of return without specifying the rationale behind the projections and included charts and graphs that were hypothetical and based on actions not yet taken. The $250,000 fine was called the largest ever enforcement of a US brokerage firm or dealer. Citigroup's CEO and its Japan CEO literally bowed in apology at the start of a news conference in Tokyo. At the news conference, they announced the closing of Cititrust & Banking Corp. that handles trust-banking and real estate banking. This closure was seen as an effort to improve the company's reputation. The CEO said that the violations that resulted in the NASD fine were the result of too aggressive sales tactics and a failure to follow its own guidelines to prevent money laundering (Morse 2004). The Japanese already were aware of and hostile to what they feel are US advertising and promotion tactics to be overly boastful and exaggerated. So, this should provide a warning to other multinationals in that market.

Further reading

See Asia Media Information and Communication Centre (AMIC) with Nanyang Technological University's School of Communication and Information, Jurong Point, PO Box 360, Singapore 916412 – annual conference papers and its bimonthly bulletin.

Corporate Reputation Watch, an annual study by Hill & Knowlton, Inc., 466 Lexington Ave, 3rd Floor, New York, NY 10017.

See also Moss and DeSanto (2002), Ricks (2000), Turk and Scanlon (2004), and a special section written by staff reporters of the *Wall Street Journal* in 2004: "A Whole New World, World Business," The Journal Report, Dow Jones, New York.

Discussion questions

1 Can you think of some communications problems you've noticed?
2 Have you ever been the victim of some cultural misunderstanding?
3 Have you ever been misunderstood by someone from another culture? What did you learn from that?
4 What do you think is the best way to avoid misunderstanding across cultures?

Research assignments

1 Find at least one example of a cultural miscommunication and explain what caused that between the two cultures involved.
2 Develop an ad for a product you like that could be placed in one other country. Explain why you think the copy and graphics would appeal to people in that country who might like and be able to buy the same things as you.

Group discussions

1 What websites do you think work best across cultures? Why?
2 What sort of persuasive appeals are almost universal? Why? Can you think of some examples you've seen?
3 Do you think serious cultural gaffes are ever truly forgiven, or forgotten? If not, why not? If so, why?
4 Can you think of any communication mistake that has caused an international incident?

Chapter 14

Developing a Worldview

The mutual confidence on which all else depends can be maintained only by an open mind and brave reliance upon free discussion. (Learned Hand, Speech at Convocation of the Board of Regents, University of the State of New York, October 24, 1952)

Objectives

- To stimulate curiosity about people and the way they live in other parts of the world.
- To encourage the investigation of other political systems, their history, and their structures.
- To ignite the quest for learning about other beliefs and customs.
- To challenge the courage to get close to other cultures.

If we are practicing in any communications field, but especially advertising/ public relations, to function efficiently in a global society we have no choice but to develop a worldview. What interferes with that is clinging to stereotypes to which we have been exposed and rejecting value systems that don't fit our own or seem to clash with our faith or our society, perhaps both.

We develop some values early from those who rear us, our schooling, our culture and our faith, or lack of a faith. We learn from experience what is acceptable in certain circumstances. For example, we learn that politics and religion are likely to create issues that can turn a conversation into a confrontation. We either stay with safe subjects or only express our opinions among those we know are most likely to agree with us. Some values come from our social and economic positions, and exposure to dramatically different social and economic situations in other countries becomes a real challenge to understand at more than a superficial level.

If you are handling communications in a dramatically different circumstance, you will have a steep and difficult learning curve to master in a very brief period of time. Your ability to learn is one of the assets you bring to public relations or advertising where you have to learn a business that may be totally unfamiliar to you in order to communicate within that professional environment and to represent that business to others effectively.

Because each of us can only react to what we see, hear and otherwise encounter in terms of our own frame of reference – which you know from Chapter 9 is created by our values and our personal experience – the broader our experiences and the more exposure we have to different sets of values, the broader the scope of our understanding. We will consider that on two levels: the personal and the professional. There are consequences at both levels for communicators operating from their own worldview, instead of a global one.

Personally

There is a tendency to seek out organizations or clients that share our values so we don't feel that we will be required to compromise our integrity. If we get in a corporate culture that demands compliance, we either change to become a "team player," get fired for not being a team player, or just leave for a more comfortable situation.

Because the CEO usually sets the tone for the corporate culture, a change in leadership may change the corporate culture. Or, the corporate culture may result in the board of directors firing the CEO because he or she isn't a "good fit" for the job. In understanding how the CEO sets the corporate culture, let's look at the role of the board of directors in hiring a CEO. The board chooses a new leader based on the direction the board wants the organization to take. In the case of mergers or acquisitions that decision is part of the negotiations that go on between the two organizations that are then approved by the two boards. The decision is critical because even when the two organizations have a similar culture, the CEO's management style will affect the way the organization functions in the future. Seldom is it smooth. If the company is publicly held, the choice always affects the stock price, based on perceptions by Wall Street analysts of what direction the market thinks the new leader will take. If the new leader is not of the same race, gender, or ethnicity as the former leader, there are additional difficulties because not all cultures are accustomed to accommodating diversity. That may be your situation also, if you have limited experience outside of your own culture.

When we are in such a challenging situation, as dealing with new leadership or a merger of cultures, it is very stressful and we are not likely to do as good a job without a broader perspective and a worldview. Communication jobs are strongly affected by management changes, especially public relations because one of the jobs is helping to establish and maintain the corporate culture. The more open the culture and the more flexible the leadership the easier it is to adjust, as long as your perspective is broad.

In one effort to broaden personal perspectives, a Jewish Peace Activist, Brenda Rosenberg, partnered with an Imam, Abdullah El Amin, director of the Council of Islamic Organizations in Michigan, to create a play to be produced by the Mosaic Youth Theatre, a 12-year-old company comprised of middle and high school students in the Detroit area. The student cast began by listening to each other's personal stories of misunderstanding, prejudice, and even persecution. After months of telling personal stories and developing trust, the young actors began improvisations to reenact the experiences they had been sharing. The dramatization of their personal stories became the foundation for a play that they helped to write and that was directed by Mosaic Theatre Founder, Rick Sperling. Rosenberg observed that while the students held different truths and different traditions, they discovered that they didn't have to change these to agree with another's and thus validate the other's perspective. Sperling noted that the basic question is whether or not people can learn to live with different versions of the truth (Schjonberg and Mack 2005).

Professionally

The second consequence of working from a limited, rather than global, worldview is professional. Organizations more inclined toward closed, rather than open, communication frequently get in trouble because they are not open to diverse points of view. You see in management and public relations advice that diversity is the key to getting enough input on policies and messages to reduce events or issues that precipitate a crisis. Diversity helps as long as dissident voices not only are tolerated, but also really heard.

Diversity means more than difference in race, gender, or ethnicity. Real diversity means respecting different value systems. When diversity within an organization is limited to assuming that one person, or even a group, represents an entire public, the risk is assigning homogeneity to a public when it doesn't and can't exist.

Just in the USA, companies have recognized a growing Hispanic population and considered them a significant part of a potential or existing market. You can't assume, though, that all Hispanics are alike. For example, try reconciling the values of Florida's Cubans with the Mexicans of Texas, and theirs with California's Chicanos and Puerto Ricans. And, that's just in the USA. Furthermore, you can't make assumptions about values when you know about someone's religion and culture. In communications, you can't fall into these traps.

You might ask if there are any basic, shared values. Former Secretary of State and UN representative Madeleine Korbel Albright thought so. In talking about the attacks on the USA on September 11, 2001, she said these forced the world to look at the role religion plays in politics, foreign policy, and everyday life. The underlying problem, Albright said, is how to harness religion's unifying potential and block its tendency to divide people and nations against themselves and others. She compared the challenge to brain surgery saying: "It's a necessary task. But it can be fatal if not done well." Albright called for all religions and nations to set domestic and foreign policies based on basic principles of valuing individual life and seeking justice for all, the tenets of all religious beliefs (Schjonberg and Mack 2005). Certainly that should be easy for three major faiths that share a common ancestor: Abraham. But major conflicts today seem to be centered on these different descendants: Jews, Moslems, and Christians.

But what if a faith is not involved? What if it is a non-faith based philosophy like China with its Confucian values, shared also by many other parts of the East Asian world? Serious discussions have gone on at a global level about what Western and Westernized nations call "human rights" in China. After the 1989 Tiananmen Square events, Europe imposed an embargo on China. The embargo has become an ethical dilemma for the European Union. Some EU members think the ban should be lifted because they see some gradual changes in China's politics.[1] In 2002, the USA made public a critical report on human rights problems in China that the Chinese government called hypocritical.

In 2005, Secretary of State Condoleezza Rice issued a report focused on efforts to improve human rights in 98 countries. China got its share of criticism for suppressing political, social, and religious groups as well as individuals. Dr. Rice acknowledged that China's amended constitution offers more protection for human rights and the nation has adopted some legal reforms for monitoring government, but the State Department report also notes that "it is unclear how or to what extent the constitutional amendment and other legal reforms will be enforced." The Bush Administration tried to influence the EU to keep the embargo, based in part on concern about the saber-rattling message of Beijing's passage

---

[1] "EU's Solana: End China Arms Ban," CNN.com [online newswire] (CNN.com: 23 March 2005); accessed April 4, 2005; available from http://www.cnn.com/2005/WORLD/Europe/03/23/eusummit/index.html

of a law authorizing the use of military forces against Taiwan.[2] This is not just a government problem. At stake are business contracts and the control over companies and nonprofit organizations operating in China and Taiwan. For public relations practitioners in these organizations and agencies who have them as clients, freedom of information is a critical factor.

What about situations when beliefs are not a factor? When priorities, instead, are political, national, and power-based? One approach has been to argue for transparency. The transparency discussion began with sources of information and the consequences for the reliability of news. Most of the "news" available globally is not a reliable version of reality from anyone's perspective. To understand that "truth," you have to be able to put it in perspective based on the source.

Summary

Social responsibility is expected of all organizations – profit making and nonprofit, whether these are multinational, transnational, national, or local. The difficulty for these organizations is determining a common ground for what is ethical and responsible behavior on a global level. Management depends on public relations counsel for evaluating policies and practices for the organization. To get sound counsel, the public relations practitioner must have a global perspective, at both the personal and professional level. According to former Principal Director of UNESCO, India, Professor Yogesh Atal (2002):

> Managing diversity . . . does not mean erasing diversity. The challenge is to locate bonds of unity in an ocean of diversity. Neither is the recipe of absorption of the outsider groups into the mainstream of society. Nor the prescription for installing insulations between the communities and encourage them to secede and close their shells a workable proposition. . . . [T]he fruits of progress are there for anyone to see. They can be used to ouster tradition and foster modernity; and they can also be used to reinforce tradition, while ushering in modernity.

Self-assessment is a major part of developing a worldview, as Box 14.1 suggests. Before you take the test in this box, though, you need to examine what you consider to be your own strengths and weaknesses, those intrinsic qualities

---

[2] "Human Rights Report Criticizes Pakistan, China," CNN.com [online newswire] (CNN.com: 28 March 2005), accessed April 4, 2005; available from: http://www.cnn.com/205/ALLPOLITICS/03/28/us.humanrights.ap/index.html

Box 14.1 Personal checklist for developing a worldview

Speak another language:	Yes	No
If "yes," how many other languages?		
Visited a country where you spoke the language used:	Yes	No
Have personal or business contacts in another country:	Yes	No
Have lived in another country:	Yes	No
Have more than one cultural heritage in your immediate family:	Yes	No
Know relatives who live in that culture from close contacts:	Yes	No
Traveled outside your country:	Yes	No
If "yes," only once?	Yes	No
Go outside your country every year?	Yes	No
Twice a year or more?	Yes	No
Know someone well who lives in another country:	Yes	No

If you have answered "no" more often than "yes," you still may have broadened your perspective through other means, such as reading. Even if you know someone well who lives outside of your country, you are more likely than many to have a better ideal of our global society.

A path for cultural literacy charted by Wendy Hall in her 1993 doctoral dissertation looks like this (the score for each item is shown on the left-hand side):

0   Our way is their way.

0   Their way is different; it's wrong.

1   Our way is "X"; their way is "Y."

2   Both their way and our way have strengths and weaknesses.

3   Cultural Synergy: We can learn from them; they can learn from us.

4   Cultural Flexibility: We can bridge differences during our interactions by adjusting our behaviors.

5   Cultural Literacy: With this partner we bridge this way; with that partner we bridge another way.

6   Cultural Mediation: We can prevent conflict, diffuse it and keep it from escalating, and resolve it where already present.

Source: Wendy Hall (1995) *Managing Cultures: Making Strategic Relationships Work*. John Wiley & Sons, New York, p. 43.

Box 14.2 Try this test too

Another self-assessment test, called the Gene Scale, developed by James W. Neuliep and J. C. McCroskey consists of 22 statements designed to measure your ethnocentricity. Self-awareness is the starting point for change.

The 22 statements are to be marked:

5   if you strongly agree
4   if you agree
3   if you are undecided
2   if you disagree
1   if you strongly disagree.

The statements are:

1 _____ Most other cultures are backward compared to my culture.
2 _____ My culture should be the role model for other cultures.
3 _____ People from other cultures act strange when they come to my culture.
4 _____ Lifestyles in other cultures are just as valid as those in my culture.
5 _____ Other cultures should try to be more like my culture.
6 _____ I'm not interested in the values and customs of other cultures.
7 _____ People in my culture could learn a lot from people in other cultures.
8 _____ Most people from other cultures just don't know what's good for them.
9 _____ I respect the values and customs of other cultures.
10 _____ Other cultures are smart to look up to our culture.
11 _____ Most people would be happier if they lived like people in my culture.
12 _____ I have many friends from different cultures.
13 _____ People in my culture have just about the best lifestyles anywhere.
14 _____ Lifestyles in other cultures are not as valid as those in my culture.
15 _____ I am very interested in the values and customs of other cultures.
16 _____ I apply my values when judging people who are different.
17 _____ I see people who are similar to me as virtuous.

---

18 _____ I do not cooperate with people who are different.
19 _____ Most people in my culture just don't know what is good for them.
20 _____ I do not trust people who are different.
21 _____ I dislike interacting with people from different cultures.
22 _____ I have little respect for the values and customs of other cultures.

For your score, follow these four steps:

Step One: Add your responses to scale items 4, 7, and 9.

Step Two: Add your responses to scale items 1, 2, 5, 8, 10, 11, 13, 14, 18, 20, 21, and 22.

Step Three: Subtract the sum from Step 1 from 18 (i.e. 18 minus your step one score).

Step Four: Add results from Step Two and Step Three.

This is your generalized ethnocentrism score.

Higher scores indicate higher ethnocentrism. Scores above 55 are considered high ethnocentrism.

Source: James W. Neuliep (2003), "Gene Scale (Self Assessment 1–3) in *Intercultural Communication: A Contextual Approach*, 2nd edn. Houghton Mifflin Co., New York, pp. 29–30. © 200 by Houghton Mifflin Co.

you came into the world with. Then look at the values you have learned, because these often direct your energies. Examine what you can do really well, and easily. Then look at what you don't do so well. You can shore up those performance weaknesses, but you may have some challenges there.

What we choose to do is generally what we do best, and improving what we don't do so well is not usually greeted with as much enthusiasm. Finally, be very tough with yourself in analyzing your relationships. How do your approaches to others and your interactions with them reflect your natural tendencies? Different behaviors can be learned, without compromising your values or standards (Levinson 2005).

Further reading

See Firoz et al. (2002), Hall (1995), Morrison et al. (1994), and Sandler (2004).

For journals, see the *Asian Journal of Communication* and the *Journal of Intercultural Research*.

Discussion questions

1 What do you think are the characteristics of a global citizen?
2 Do you know any? Who are they? How did you meet them?
3 Which parts of the world do you think you know least about?
4 If you had a job that sent you to live outside of your country for a year or more, where would you want to go? Why?

Research assignments

1 National Public Radio has a program that includes a "geo quiz" in which hints are given about a place, usually some place that has been in the news recently, but not always. Do some research and develop a "geo quiz" that offers interesting hints about a place, tips that would be particular only to that place. Include five questions and their answers.
2 Assume that you have been given a scholarship to study abroad, all expenses paid. Choose a university and find out all you can about it and the region in which it is located. Write your letter of application explaining why you want to study there.

Group discussions

1 In your group, how many people have lived or visited another country and can share an observation, experience, or incident that gave them special insight into life there.
2 What classes in your educational experience so far has provoked your curiosity about other parts of the world? How?
3 Do you listen to, watch television programming, or read newspapers from other parts of the world? Which media, and why do you choose them?
4 Outside of your own country are there some artists (from any art form) whose careers you follow or whose works you enjoy? Who? What country? What is it that interests you about them or their work? Has that influenced the way you think about their country?

References

Amienyi, O. P. (2004) "Anatomy of a Pro-Development Television Program: The Integrative Content of Kenya KBC-TV's 'Face to Face,'" *International Communication Bulletin*, Vol. 39, No. 3–4 (Fall), pp. 12–23.

Ang Peng Hwa (2004) "A Model of Internet Rule Development: A Case Study of Liability for Third-Party Content," *Media Asia*, Vol. 31, No. 3, pp. 133–9. A note in the journal says the paper is a chapter from Ang Peng Hwa's book, *Ordering Chaos: Regulating the Internet* (2005) Thomason Learning Asia.

Arbib, M. A. (2005) "Neuroinformatics," *The Human Brain*, Phi Kappa Phi Forum, Vol. 85, No. 1 (Winter/Spring), pp. 34–39.

Atal, Y. (2002) "Managing Diversity in a Multicultural Society," *Media Asia*, Vol. 29, No. 2, pp. 63–6, 70, 111.

Ball, D., Ellison, S., Adams, J. and Fowler, G. A. (2004) "Recipes without Borders?" *Wall Street Journal*, August 18, pp. B1, 3.

Bardhan, M. and Patwardhan, P. (2004) "Multinational Corporations and Public Relations in a Historically Resistant Host Culture," *Journal of Communication Management*, Vol. 8, No. 3, pp. 246–63.

Begley, S. (2004) "Racism Studies Find Rational Part of Brain Can Override Prejudice," Science Journal, *Wall Street Journal*, November 19, 2004, p. B1.

Biagi, S. and Foxworth, M. K.-F. (1997) *Facing Difference: Race, Gender and Mass Media*. Pine Forge Press, A Sage Publications Company, Thousand Oaks, CA.

Bremner, J. D. (2005) "Does Stress Damage the Brain?" *The Human Brain*, Phi Kappa Phi Forum, Vol. 85, No. 1 (Winter/Spring), pp. 27–29.

Burgoon, J. K. and White, C. H. (1997) "Researching Message Production: A View from Interactive Adaptation Theory." In: Greene, J. O. (ed.) *Message Production: Advances in Communication Theory*. Lawrence Erlbaum Associates, Mahwah, NJ.

Carter, P. and Russell, K. (2003) *More Psychometric Testing: 1000 New Ways to Assess Your Personality, Creativity, Intelligence and Lateral Thinking*, John Wiley & Sons, Hoboken, NJ.

Chatterjee, D. K. (2004) *The Ethics of Assistance*. Cambridge University Press, New York.

Chebel, M. (2003) *Symbols of Islam*. Barnes & Noble Books, New York.

Cheng, J. (2005) "China Demands Concrete Proof of Ad Claims," *Wall Street Journal*, July 8, pp. B1, 4.

Culbertson, H. C. and Chen, N. (eds.) (1996) *International Public Relations: A Comparative Analysis*. Lawrence Erlbaum, Mahwaw, NJ.

Dainton, M. and Zelley, E. D. (2005) *Applying Communication Theory for Professional Life: A Practical Introduction*. Thousand Oaks, CA: Sage.

Dawes, M. (2004) "Challenging Culturally-Expected Ways of Thinking," *ETC: A Review of General Semantics*, Vol. 61, No. 4, pp. 72–4.

De Beer, A. S., and Merrill, J. C. (eds.) *Global Journalism: Topical Issues and Media Systems*, 4th ed. Pearson Allyn and Bacon, Boston, MA.

de Bono, E. (1971) *Lateral Thinking for Management: A Handbook of Creativity*, American Management Association, New York; www.edwdebono.co.jp

DeCarlo, S. (2005) "The World's Leading Companies," *Forbes*, April 18, Vol. 175, No. 8, pp. 164–208.

DeFleur, M. L. and Ball-Rokeach, S. (1989) *Theories of Mass Communication*, 5th ed. Longman, New York.

Delaney, K. J. and Trachtenberg, J. A. (2005) "Publishers Challenge Google's Book-Scanning Efforts: Lawsuit Says Digital Copies Infringe on Copyright Laws; A Replay of Music Battle?" *Wall Street Journal*, October 20, pp. A1, 6.

Duncan, T. (2002) *IMC, Integrated Marketing Communication*. McGraw-Hill, New York.

El-Astal, Mohammed A. S. (2005) "Culture Influence on Educational Public Relations Officers' Ethical Judgments, *Public Relations Review*, Vol. 31, No. 3, pp. 362–75.

Feemster, R. (2004) "Found in Translation" and "A Guide to Ethnic Media," *FFR: Ford Foundation Report*, Spring 2004, Vol. 35, No. 2, pp. 4–5.

Ferguson, Y. H. and Mansbach, R. W. (2004) *Remapping Global Politics*. Cambridge University Press, New York.

Firoz, N. M., Maghrabi, A. S., and Kim, K. H. (2002) "Think Globally, Manage Culturally," *International Journal of Communication Management*, Vol. 12, No. 3, pp. 32–49.

Freedman, A. M. (2000) "As Unicef Battles Baby-Formula Makers, African Infants Sicken," *Wall Street Journal*, December 5, pp. A1 and 18.

Friedman, K. (2005) "Culture Club: Tips for Speaking With International Audiences." In *Public Relations Tactics*, Public Relations Society of America, New York, Vol. 12, No. 2.

Friedman, T. L. (2005) *The World Is Flat: A Brief History of the Twenty-First Century*. Farrar, Straus and Giroux, New York.

Funkhouser, G. R. (1973) "Trends in Media Coverage of Issues of the '60s," *Journalism Quarterly* (Winter) 50, pp. 533–8.

Gould, C. C. (2004) *Globalizing Democracy and Human Rights*. Cambridge University Press, New York.

Grosswiler, P. (2004) "Continuing Media Controversies." In: De Beer, A. S. and Merrill, J. C. (eds.) *Global Journalism: Topical Issues and Media Systems*, 4th ed. Pearson Allyn and Bacon, Boston, MA, pp. 113–15.

Gugliotta, G. (2002–3) "When Did Writing Begin?" *Washington Post*, National Weekly Edition, December 23, 2002–January 5, 2003, p. 35.

Hall, E. T. (1959) "Introduction." *The Silent Language*. Garden City, NY: Doubleday.

Hall, W. (1995) *Managing Cultures: Making Strategic Relationships Work.* John Wiley & Sons, New York.

Ho, Fei-Wen and Hallahan, K. (2004) "Post-earthquake Crisis Communications in Taiwan: An Examination of Corporate Advertising and Strategy Motives," *Journal of Communication Management*, Vol. 8, No. 3, pp. 291–306.

Jean, G. (1998) *Signs, Symbols and Ciphers: Decoding the Message.* Thames and Hudson, London.

Johnson, I. (2005) "Conflicting Advice: Islamic Justice Finds A Foothold in the Heart of Europe, *Wall Street Journal*, August 4, pp. A1, 8.

Johnson, K. (2005) "Spain Tries to Get Macho Men to Lift a Finger on Washday," *Wall Street Journal*, October 1–2, pp. A1, 6.

Kruckeberg, D. and Tsetsura, K. (2004) "International Journalism Ethics." In: De Beer, A. S. and Merrill, J. C. (eds.) *Global Journalism: Topical Issues and Media Systems*, 4th ed. Pearson Allyn and Bacon, Boston, MA, p. 92.

LeGall, R. (2003) *Symbols of Catholicism.* Barnes & Noble Books, New York.

Levenson, C. B. (2000) *Symbols of Tibetan Buddhism.* Barnes & Noble Books, New York.

Levinson, M. H. (2005) "Using General Semantics for Effective Self-Management," *ETC: A Review of General Semantics*, Vol. 62, No. 4 (October), pp. 370–80.

Littlejohn, S. W. (2002) *Theories of Human Communication*, 7th ed. Wadsworth/ Thomson Learning, Belmont, CA.

Lutz, W. (1996) *The New Doublespeak: Why No One Knows What Anyone's Saying Anymore.* HarperCollins, New York.

Mack, J. (2003) *The Museum of the Mind: Art and Memory of World Cultures.* British Museum Press, London.

McKenzie, R. (2005) *Comparing Media from Around the World.* Allyn & Bacon/Longman Publishers, Boston, MA.

Merrill, J. C. (1997) *Journalism Ethics.* St. Martin's Press, New York.

Merrill, J. C. (2004) "International Media Systems: An Overview." In: De Beer, A. S. and Merrill, J. C. (eds.) *Global Journalism: Topical Issues and Media Systems*, 4th ed. Pearson Allyn and Bacon, Boston, MA, pp. 19–34.

Mitchell, R. (2004) "Speaking a Universal Language," *PR Week*, August 9, p. 18.

Molleda, J. C. and Ferguson, M. A. (2004) "Public Relations Roles in Brazil: Hierarchy Eclipses Gender Differences," *Journal of Public Relations Research*, Vol. 16, No. 4, pp. 327–51.

Morrison, T., Conaway, W. A., and Borden, G. A. (1994) *Kiss, Bow or Shake Hands.* Adams Media Group, Avon, MA.

Morse, A. (2004) "Citigroup Extends Apology to Japan," *Wall Street Journal*, October 26, pp. A3, 16.

Moss, D. and DeSanto, B. (2002) *Public Relations Cases: International Perspectives.* Routledge, London.

Neuliep, J. W. (2003) *Intercultural Communication: A Contextual Approach*, 2nd ed. Houghton Mifflin, New York.

Newsom, D. (2002) "Disconnects? Working with PR Colleagues across Borders when Public Relations Jobs Are Different." In: Biberman, J. and Alkhafaji, A. (eds.) *Business*

Research Yearbook Global Business Perspectives, Vol. 9, International Academy of Business Disciplines, pp. 703–7.

Newsom, D. (2004a) "Global Advertising and Public Relations." In: De Beer, A. S. and Merrill, J. C. (eds.) *Global Journalism: Topical Issues and Media Systems*, 4th ed. Pearson Allyn and Bacon, Boston, MA, pp. 93–111.

Newsom, D. (2004b) "Singapore Poised for Prominence in Public Relations among Emerging Democracies." In: Tilson, D. J. and Alozie, E. C. (eds.) *Toward the Common Good: Perspectives in International Public Relations*, Pearson Allyn and Bacon, Boston, MA, pp. 363–86.

Newsom, D. (2007) "PR Ethics and Responsibilities." In: Newsom, D., Turk, J. V., and Kruckeberg, D. *This Is PR: The Realities of Public Relations*, 9th ed. Wadsworth/ Thomson, Belmont, CA, pp. 168–70.

Newsom, D., Turk, J. V., and Kruckeberg, D. (2007) *This Is PR: The Realities of Public Relations*, 9th ed. Wadsworth/Thomson, Belmont, CA.

Nisbett, R. E. (2003) *The Geography of Thought: How Asians and Westerners Think Differently . . . and Why*. Simon & Schuster, New York.

Nystrom, C. L. (2002) "Immediate Man: The Symbolic Environment of Fanaticism," *ETC: A Review of General Semantics*, Vol. 59, No. 1, p. 179.

O'Keefe, J. (1998) *Business Beyond the Box*. Nicholas Brealey Publishing, Yarmouth, ME.

O'Keefe, K. (2005) *Quill* Magazine, September, pp. 14–15.

Ouaknin, M. (2000) *Symbols of Judaism*. Barnes & Noble Books, New York.

Park, J. (2001) "Images of 'Ho Bo' and PR in Korean Newspapers," *Public Relations Review*, Vol. 27, No. 4, pp. 237–54.

Parker, G. and Lublin, J. S. (2004) "More Japanese May Rethink Loyalty to Jobs," *Wall Street Journal*, August 18, pp. B1, 3.

Reus-Smit, C. (2004) *The Politics of International Law*. Cambridge University Press, New York.

Ricks, D. A. (2000) *Blunders in International Communication*, 3rd ed. Blackwell, Malden, MA.

Samovar, L. A. and Porter, R. E. (2003) *Communication between Cultures*, 5th ed. Wadsworth Thomson Learning, Belmont, CA.

Sandler, T. (2004) *Global Collective Action*. Cambridge University Press, New York.

Schimmelfennig, F. (2004) *The EU, NATO and the Integration of Europe*. Cambridge University Press, New York.

Schjonberg, M. F. and Mack, D. (2005) "Stop Religious Divisions," *Episcopal Life*, Vol. 14, No. 4 (April).

Seligman, D. (2005) "Liberty, European-Style: The EU Has Funny Ideas about Human Rights. For example, the idea that free speech is not among those rights," *Forbes*, April 25, pp. 97–8.

Sesit, M. R. (2005) "Geopolitical Risk: History's Constant," *Wall Street Journal*, August 4, 2005, p. C12.

Severin, W. J. and Tankard, J. W. Jr. (2001) *Communication Theories: Origins, Methods and Uses in the Mass Media*, 5th ed. New York: Addison Wesley Longman.

References

Shlachter, B. (2000) "Anatomy of a Recall: Science Creates a Crisis in Corn," *Fort Worth Star Telegram*, December 31, pp. F1, 7.

Springston, J. K. and Champion, V. L. (2004) "Public Relations and Cultural Aesthetics: Designing Health Brochures," *Public Relations Review*, Vol. 30, pp. 483–91.

Sriramesh, K. and Verčič, D. (2003) *The Global Public Relations Handbook: Theory, Research and Practice*. Lawrence Erlbaum, Mahwah, NJ.

Stevenson, R. L. (2004) "Freedom of the Press around the World." In: De Beer, A. S. and Merrill, J. C. (eds.) *Global Journalism: Topical Issues and Media Systems*, 4th ed. Pearson Allyn and Bacon, Boston, MA, pp. 66–83.

Tilson, D. J. and Alozie, E. C. (eds.) (2004) *Toward the Common Good: Perspectives in International Public Relations*. Pearson, New York.

Tsetsura, K. (2005) "Communication Leaders in Poland Decry Media Bribery, But Say It Occurs Often in Their Country," www.instituteforpr.com

Turk, J. V. S. and Scanlan, L. H. (2004) *The Evolution of Public Relations: Case Studies from Countries in Transition*, 2nd ed. The Institute for Public Relations Research and Education, Gainesville, FL.

Varner, I. and Beamer, L. (2001) *Intercultural Communication in the Global Workplace*. McGraw Hill, New York.

Wanta, W., Golan, G. and Lee, C. (2004) "Agenda Setting and International News: Media Influence on Public Perceptions of Foreign Nations," *Journalism and Mass Communication Quarterly*, Vol. 81, No. 2, Summer, pp. 364–77.

Ward, S. J. A. (2005) "Philosophical Foundations for Global Journalism Ethics," *Journal of Mass Media Ethics*, Vol. 20, No. 1, pp. 3–21.

Weaver, D. H. (2004) "Journalists, International Profiles," In: De Beer, A. S. and Merrill, J. C. (eds.) *Global Journalism: Topical Issues and Media Systems*, 4th ed. Pearson Allyn and Bacon, Boston, MA.

Wrighton, J. and Sapsford, J. (2005) "Split Shift for Nissan's Rescuer, Ghosn, New Road Rules Await at Renault," *Wall Street Journal*, April 26, pp. A1, 10.

Yuan, L. (2004) "Web Site Helps Chinese in U.S. Navigate Life," *Wall Street Journal*, October 26, pp. B1–2.

Index

Index

Index

Index

Bridging the Gaps in Global Communication